No one, absolutely no one, has the experience, training, and wisdom to uncover the forces behind the school shootings like Bob Larson. If parents and educators had read this book before Columbine, it might never have taken place. May the tragedy of Columbine birth change in our lives. It will if we read this amazing book!

PETER LOWE
CEO, Peter Lowe International
Creator of "The Success Seminars"

If you have children in school, you need this book. If you have friends who have children in school, you need to buy and give them this book. Bob Larson's book equips us with the tools to protect our beloved children from both physical and spiritual harm. I've know this talented man for a decade. I'm a better father to our six-year-old son because of Bob. You, too, will be a better parent after reading this book.

JACK THOMPSON
Miami attorney representing families of
Paducah, Kentucky, shooting victims

EXTREME EVIL:
Kids
Killing Kids

BOB LARSON

A JANET THOMA BOOK

THOMAS NELSON PUBLISHERS
/ Nashville

Published in Nashville, Tennessee, by Thomas Nelson, Inc.

Unless otherwise noted, Scripture quotations are from the NEW KING JAMES VERSION. Copyright © 1979, 1980, 1982, Thomas Nelson, Inc., Publishers.

Scripture quotations noted TLB are from *The Living Bible,* copyright © 1971. Used by permission of Tyndale House Publishers, Inc., Wheaton, Illinois 60189. All rights reserved.

Library of Congress Cataloging-in-Publication Data

Larson, Bob
    Extreme evil: kids killing kids / Bob Larson
      p. cm.
    ISBN 0-7852-6870-7 (pbk.)
    1. School shootings—United States. 2. School violence—United States. 3. Students—Crime against—United States. I. Title.
    LB3013.3.L37 1999
    371.7'8—dc21
                                           99-43087
                                              CIP

Printed in the United States of America
1 2 3 4 5 6 QPV 04 03 02 01 00 99

DEDICATION

This book is dedicated to my wife and two children. They gave up important family time for me to write this book in a rush. My prayer is that the hours we missed being together will be multiplied many times over with providential blessings.

CONTENTS

ACKNOWLEDGMENTS

The young men and women who bravely faced the Columbine killers. I apologize in advance for any, known only to God, whose testimony of courage I failed to recognize. Through sweat and tears I wrote this book, but with their blood these young martyrs reminded us all of the ultimate price of faith.

PART ONE

EXTREME EVIL

CHAPTER 1

THE COLUMBINE KILLINGS

She didn't answer my question. She stood there silently. The index finger of her right hand slowly etched a watery trail on the rain-soaked trunk of the old maroon V6L Acura Legend. It was an almost hypnotic exercise that I sensed was a way of ignoring the pain she was feeling.

"Do you know who this car belonged to?"

She nodded.

"Will you tell me?"

"No," she whispered silently.

The drizzle drowned the hundreds of bouquets that had been piled on top of the car. The young woman's friends wanted to preserve what they could of the memorial. I paused as several of them struggled to erect a canopy over the car. One hammered pegs into the muddy earth in front of the vehicle. Another secured the tent's supporting poles nearest the rear of the car by securing the pegs with weights.

"Is your refusal to answer my question a way of not admitting she's dead?"

The teenager nodded again.

I spoke softly. "I understand. You probably feel like just

speaking her name somehow acknowledges that she's really gone."

The young woman's moist brown eyes looked directly at me. "She parked her car here in this same spot every day. Now she'll never . . ." Her voice trailed off.

I put my arm around her as she dissolved into tears.

This scene took place less than forty-eight hours after the April 20, 1999, killings at Columbine High School in Littleton, Colorado—America. The media had barely begun to get a grip on the immensity of the tragedy. But it was trying.

Behind me, thirty satellite uplink trucks beamed the news of Littleton to the world. Reporters speaking a dozen languages milled about, capturing sound bites from the handful of dazed students who held court on their thoughts. Immaculately coiffured female news anchors and their blow-dried coanchors primped in front of mirrors as they prepared to face the cameras. Scores of video crews scurried about to position themselves for the next interview with any student wearing a Columbine High School jacket. It seemed as if the emotional center of the world was right here, right now, on this muddy space of earth, staked out a few hundred yards away from the school building.

But the spiritual center of the universe was that maroon Acura. In the next few days, that car, which had belonged to Rachel Scott, age seventeen, would be smothered by a thousand or more plastic encased clutches of flowers. It was a way for students and the public to say, "Rachel, we'll never forget you."

They wanted to remember Rachel, but they wanted to forget what had happened. She was one of two teenage girls, among the twelve slaughtered students, who died for their faith. Like her classmate Cassie Bernall, Rachel gave a truth-ful answer to the question, "Do you believe in God?"

Why was that question so important to the shooters?

That's one reason I'm writing this book. Unlike others who watched what went on through the eyes of Katie Couric or Dan Rather, who jetted across the country to report from the scene, I drove ten minutes from my Denver-based office to be on-site and find out what really motivated the killers. Much of what I discovered wasn't reported in the secular press. They were too busy trumpeting headlines that repeat-edly asked the same question, typified by the bold print on the cover of *Newsweek*'s May 3, 1999, special edition: "WHY?"

The answer is easy, if we want to know it. If you don't know the answer, you'll find it in this book. But you'll find more. I intend to point fingers. I'll assign blame. I'll tell you exactly why this happened and who is responsible. And I'll go beyond that. I'll shame those who have silently profited over the dead bodies of our children.

Two weeks after the tragedy, President Bill Clinton called a White House Strategy Session on Children, Violence, and Responsibility to discuss the Columbine killings and what could be done to prevent them from happening again. The short version of the president's conclusion was this: "We're all to blame. We're all responsible."

No! A thousand times no!

We're not all culpable, and neither are millions of fine God-fearing families. Some kids don't wear trench coats to school. They don't idolize Hitler. They don't indulge in vio-lent video games, and they don't sit unsupervised in front of a television set for five hours a day. They don't listen to gangsta rap music and they don't go to movies like *The*

Matrix. They don't build bombs in our garages without their parents knowing it.

There's a reason they don't do these things. Their parents care. The parents oversee their children's welfare and account for their conduct. The parents know where their kids are, who they're with, and what they're doing. Most importantly, religion isn't a postscript for their lives. These parents do everything they can to inculcate values that extol nonviolence, love, and the worth of every living soul.

But not every parent or concerned adult reading this book may be so fortunate. Some are recent converts to faith, and their past experiences of child-rearing may have sown seeds to be reaped. Others have friends and loved ones whose children are at risk and want to know how to reach them. Some are community and church leaders who need to know the signs that make a kid into a killer. And there is always the possibility that some good family of faith has a wayward child. In spite of every effort to the contrary, he or she insists on being rebellious.

That's why this book isn't about perfect parenting. It's about what we can do and should do to perfect our parenting. It's about understanding our age and confronting the culture that kills our kids. Most of all it's about any kid anywhere who may be the next to pull the trigger. The violence can end if we want it to and have the will to do it.

WHY THEY KILLED AT COLUMBINE

I live in Colorado, and this time of year is usually bright and sunny, but today the air was cold and damp, the mud was deep, and the clouds were heavy. This plot of earth was the closest place authorities could find to establish a staging ground for the hordes of media equipment and personnel. Makeshift tents were everywhere. The world was watching.

Some tents protected electronic equipment and shielded the on-camera personalities from the steady drizzle. Other tents covered small patches of land where students and friends had left mementos. Balloons of Columbine High School colors floated in the piercing wind. Flower petals wilted under the fresh snow that had fallen overnight. The memorials included pictures of the slain students and hundreds of handwritten messages.

A white board read: "Our prayers and thoughts are with you. We will get through this together."

A tattered piece of notebook paper declared: "Romans 3:23—for all have sinned and fallen short of the glory of God."

Someone named Heather had drawn an angel with the caption, "You're all angels now."

Several football jerseys, bearing the numbers of fallen classmates, hung from hastily erected tripods.

A large piece of cardboard, encased in plastic to protect it from the elements, read: "Dear Heavenly Father, the devil is at work here and we need your power to help fight him. Help the injured and heal them. I beg of you, Father, let no more die!"

In the midst of such moving mementos, the media personnel did their jobs with detached precision. Some traded "war" stories. "Didn't I see you at Hurricane George?" one man asked another. "I remember you from Honduras," another recalled. They had lots to do. CNN, CBS, ABC, NBC, CNBC, and Fox network logos branded the jackets of several hundred men and women stringing cable and positioning cameras.

I moved toward a section of the area where various students were being interviewed. "Everybody liked Isaiah," said a fifteen-year-old named Matt, referring to Isaiah Shoels, the African-American student who was killed. "My cousin saw it happen. The shooters saw Isaiah underneath a table and said, 'Look, N——!' Then they shot him in the side of the head. My cousin saw the bullet go in his head and out again."

The young man burst into tears. "The trench-coat mafia," he went on after regaining his composure, "were always threatening me and my friends. They'd call my Mexican friends Spics. But they had Chinese friends. I don't understand that." He paused as his mind wandered. Then he abruptly shifted thoughts. "None of us has ever seen anyone dead before. We've never seen that much blood before."

Matt broke down again. Slowly I made my way toward another group who were standing by themselves with no reporters in sight. As I drew near, I heard one of them say, "They claimed to be vampires." That piqued my attention.

"Excuse me," I said, entering their circle. "Who was a vampire?"

"The trench-coat guys," a girl named Susie said. "One of them—I'm not sure who it was, Harris, Klebold, or one of their group—told me he was actually afraid of the light."

"Yeah, and they were into Wicca," a boy named Eric chimed in. "Why doesn't the #@** press talk about that?"

The string of profanities that proceeded from his mouth convinced me he wasn't a Christian, so he had no religious bias to cause him to make that kind of statement. I looked directly at him.

"I always knew they were in some kind of cult," Eric

went on. "They practiced the religion of Wicca. You'd see books on Wicca in their backpacks all the time. Hey, if that's what they worship, let that be their religion . . ."

His voice trailed off for a moment, and then he talked more about the trench-coat mafia and their fascination with Wicca. Most people who refer to witchcraft call it witchcraft, not Wicca. The distinction between the two was critical. The more I heard the group talk of vampirism and witchcraft, I realized how little any of them really knew about the actual practices of both. So their referring to it as Wicca was significant; it stemmed directly from the fact that the books Harris, Klebold, and their buddies were reading were textbooks about Wicca, the more serious name for witchcraft preferred by those who are doing more than dabbling.

"So, why do you think they did what they did?"

Eric uttered an expletive, taking God's name in vain, his anger coming through clearly. His blasphemous adjectives were incongruously followed by the answer to my question.

"Witchcraft! That's the only reason they would think and act in such a dark kind of way. They were homosexuals too, or at least that's what most kids thought. Maybe they weren't, but they were called that."

I moved away from Eric and Susie toward another group of four, two boys and two girls, standing by themselves, each smoking one cigarette after another. "Can I ask you a couple of questions?"

"Sure," a girl named Debra with blonde hair said, almost sarcastically. She puffed a cigarette incessantly, tipping her head back and blowing huge puffs of smoke in the air.

"Some other kids say that Harris and Klebold were gay,

that they were involved in vampirism and witchcraft, that Marilyn Manson . . ."

"That's not true!" Debra shot back at me. I had obviously hit a raw nerve.

"They were just kids dying for attention. Klebold was the smartest kid I knew. I used to copy off his paper," she continued.

"So why did they do it?"

"Four-twenty! They wanted to go out with a bang."

"Four-twenty?" I asked.

"Yeah, four-twenty, April 20, International Pot Day. It's a big holiday around here. It's a day everybody comes together and celebrates the good times by smoking pot. A day of partying. Now Harris and Klebold have ruined it. It'll never be the same again."

I cringed. I was angry. All around me were reminders of the carnage of Columbine High School. People were dead. Lives had been shattered forever. Families were suffering the loss of loved ones. And all this selfish stoner could think of was smoking dope.

I kept my cool for the sake of further inquiry. "Did you ever use drugs with Harris and Klebold?"

The other three joined Debra in an affirmative response. "Hey, I went to elementary school with Dylan Klebold," the other girl, Ruth, said. "I've known him forever, and he's always been, like, this weird kid. I've smoked dope with him. Harris too. All of us have."

"Do any of you see the connection between the antisocial philosophy that drove Harris and Klebold to kill, and the fact you all used drugs?" I asked.

Once again the anger of these kids surfaced.

"No way," one of the boys answered.

"But smoking dope is illegal. You're breaking the law," I insisted. "And when you break one law, what's to keep you from breaking another?"

None of them spoke, but their body language was plain. They resented the connection I made and thought I was stupid for even suggesting the idea that doing drugs could lead to more dangerous behavior. Then one of the guys made a startling admission.

"See, when you do drugs, you isolate yourself from people and lose touch with reality," he said. "The change is so subtle you don't realize you're psycho, and you don't know it because you're secluded from everybody in the normal world."

With a concession like that, there wasn't much more for me to say, except, "I suppose you'll all go smoke a joint to forget about all of this."

Ruth looked at me seriously. "No, I haven't smoked weed since it happened. I guess that's my way of paying tribute— by cooling out a little bit."

What is to be made of these conversations? First, that even in the midst of such an immense tragedy, some youth today are so overcome by their hedonistic lifestyles that their only concern is the next big thrill, the next drug, the next party. Jesus Christ himself could appear to them, and it wouldn't make a difference in their behavior.

Second, the evidence that Harris and Klebold were heavily influenced by drugs, homosexuality, vampirism, and witchcraft is admittedly hearsay. But I heard these same themes repeated again and again by other students who knew them, those who had no reason to tack part of the blame on these aberrant forms of behavior. In fact, none of the students to whom I spoke saw these forms of behavior as

11

objectionable. Rather, such actions were stated matter-of-factly, like it was no big deal these kid killers were described in such a way.

That in itself was disturbing. The very things that may have been at least part of the reason these kids killed weren't taken seriously. The evidence was right in front of these young people, and they couldn't see it. Neither could the press. They were more interested in body counts, police briefings, and psychological theories than moral issues.

My opinion of the cause, after I've talked to scores of Columbine students and considered all the evidence? Homosexuality? It is likely—at least bisexuality was involved—but inconclusive. Vampirism? Probably a momentary indulgence, one of a potpourri of antisocial activities that further fueled the fires of rebellion. Witchcraft? Yes, but how deeply, no one seems to know. Harris and Klebold kept a lot of things to themselves. Drugs? Absolutely. All of these elements are key to understanding the denial that took over their minds and made their actions so inhumane, so detached.

THEY WERE THERE

They spoke with me on condition of anonymity. They told me things that were never reported in the press. They were professionals, some of the first to enter Columbine High School after the S.W.A.T. team had given the okay. They were there to comfort the frightened, to take pictures of what happened, and to record crime scene evidence. And a year or so from now, a significant number of them won't be doing these same jobs any more. That's the way such modern tragedies affect those who are called upon to sort out the slaughter. (Remember the often-reproduced picture of that fireman carrying a baby out of the rubble of the Oklahoma City Federal Building bombing? He's dead now. Suicide.)

I wanted to know what it was like to walk inside Columbine High School with fresh blood still flowing on the floor and the smell of explosives still hanging in the air. From what I was told, it wasn't at all what I had imagined.

"Deathly quiet." Sure, you've heard that phrase before. But there seemed to be no other way to adequately describe the crime scene. Quiet, *deathly* quiet. That's what they told me. Schools are places of noise—laughter, lockers slamming, the sounds of kids yelling at one another, hundreds of heavy footsteps racing toward class—all that was missing.

"The silence was deafening." Yes, it's an overused phrase, but that's the best way they could depict what it was like walking from room to room, checking out bodies and sorting through evidence. Detectives in hushed tones made notes on handheld recorders. Photographers knelt almost reverently to record how the bodies were lying, at what angles the bullets entered, and how the killing had taken place.

"Did you sense the evil?" I asked someone.

"No." I was surprised by the answer. It seemed to me there would have been a lingering sense of the sinister. "Whatever evil had been there was gone. It had done its job, and there was nothing more to do, so it just moved on."

That more complete explanation made sense. After all, Harris and Klebold were dead, and whatever demons had driven them to such horror had moved on to fresh fodder.

The first question asked at the police debriefings that took place outside after those who first entered had exited was: "What did you see?"

My sources told me: "You get facts by asking what people saw. On the scene of a trauma, you never ask how people feel. In a time of tragedy, 70 percent of what people express is emotional."

Where was God when all this happened? That's a fair question. But it's also just as honest to ask, "What else might have happened except for the grace of God?"

Think about those unexploded propane tanks. One early team that entered the building started to walk into the cafeteria where two twenty-pound tanks were rigged to detonate. The team stopped for no reason; they just didn't go in. How many more might have died if they had? Truly, only God knows.

The shooters had fired at these bombs in an attempt to set them off, but they didn't explode. No expert I talked to had a reason why. "Maybe an angel deflected the bullets so more wouldn't be killed," one person commented. "If those bombs had gone off, the whole building and everyone in it would have been destroyed," the expert stated. Maybe the metaphysical explanation wasn't so far from the truth.

What about Harris and Klebold? I spoke with those who saw the bodies. For reasons associated with the investigation I can't divulge all that was told me. But I can say this. Those who looked at the lifeless forms of these two teenagers were struck by how normal and clean-cut they looked. Underneath the trench coats they were nicely dressed. They didn't look like killers. Most murderers have a certain look about them. I understand, because I've counseled death-row inmates. I know what those who gazed down on the bodies of Harris and Klebold were talking about when they said, "These kids weren't the kind who would kill."

More revealing was the observation, "Whatever was 'in' them wasn't there anymore."

How had this affected those professionals who were closest to what happened? "The entire law enforcement community is heavy with unexplained questions," I was told. "And so are most people in Littleton," I was quick to reply.

THE CHRISTIANS WHO WERE KILLED

Two of the victims of the Columbine killings, Rachel Scott and Cassie Bernall, have come to symbolize all that is hopeful about the redemptive power of tragedy. Millions of Americans wept as they remembered the martyrdom of these brave young women. I will forever have the sight of Rachel's car burned into my mind. What impressed me the most was not the thousands of bouquets that buried it or the television satellite uplink trucks parked around it. It was the empty driver's seat.

According to the Columbine students I spoke with, Rachel parked her car every day in the same lot and at the same spot. I can imagine her the morning of April 20, 1999, exiting the car with a stack of books under one arm and the other arm reaching through the strap of a backpack to sling it over her shoulder. What was different about that morning? Nothing at the time, to Rachel. But to heaven, it was the hour of welcoming. A soldier of the faith was about to walk, not into the front doors of Columbine High, but into the arms of Jesus.

"Do you believe in God?"

Those who witnessed her murder aren't sure which killer, Klebold or Harris, asked the question. They just remember hearing the shot, and then watching Rachel clutch her wounded leg and fall to the ground.

"Do you believe in God?"

That question will never be forgotten by the youth who have come to revere the memory of Rachel and Cassie. Rachel's quiet response, "Yes," was followed by the shot heard around the world.

"Then go to be with Him now!" was the grim response from the lips of the kid killer, his eyes glazed with hate.

Whether Rachel or Cassie was first, no one seems to remember. But the question to Cassie was the same. "Do you believe in God?"

Cassie wasn't shot before being confronted about her faith, like Rachel was, so her answer was perhaps more poignant. Accounts of exactly what she said differ, but at least one version has her giving an invitation for her killer to turn from his murderous intent: "There is a God, and you need to accept Jesus Christ."

Most versions of Cassie's last words have her simply stating, "Yes, I believe in God."

Whatever the actual affirmations of Cassie and Rachel may have been, the faith of these two brave Christians has caused millions of other youth—and adults—to wonder, *What would I have said? Would I have given witness to my faith in Christ as courageously?* Youth pastors across the country have reported an upsurge in religious fervor among the young.

That silent teen who stood by Rachel Scott's car, whose story I used to introduce this book, dared not speak the names of Columbine's victims, but millions of spiritually challenged youth now proclaim their names, and their witness, with enthusiasm. "Yes, I also believe!" they affirm.

"They died for their faith. I must be willing to do the same."

As I write, I'm surrounded by piles of newspaper clippings, audio- and videotapes, and stacks of paper, all representing the exhaustive research I've compiled to write this book. But no piece of paper is more precious to me than a copy of a beautifully penned page from Cassie Bernall's diary. Her friends believe this was her last testament. The Sunday before she was shot, Cassie wrote down her thoughts about her relationship to Christ. This courageous young woman had found her way out of drugs and involvement in witchcraft to the cross of Christ. Not knowing that she had mere days before her life would be violently ended, she copied in her diary the following verses from *The Living Bible:*

> Now I have given up on everything else—I have found it to be the only way to really know Christ and to experience the mighty power that brought Him back to life again, and to find out what it really means to suffer and to die with Him. So, whatever it takes, I will be one who lives in the fresh newness of life of those who are alive from the dead. (Phil. 3:10–11 TLB)

Anyone who has observed the revivalistic fervor after Columbine has to be impressed by the numerous stories of the spiritual legacy of Cassie and Rachel. Before a soccer match at a school nearby Littleton, an uncommon occurrence took place as the athletes assembled. With the massacre of Columbine still obviously fresh on his mind, one of the players stepped to the public address microphone. Recalling how Columbine students had gathered unashamedly to pray in the hours after the killings, the student spoke. "Can we all stop for a moment to pray?" he said. "Maybe if we pray now, we won't have to later."

The work of God in the lives of those devastated by the horror of Littleton has struck a responsive chord in the lives of millions of others. While greedy adults continue to rape our civilization in the name of free speech, a new, more conservative generation is on the rise. They've been told that there is no truth, and they can plainly see where that has led. They've been taught there is no God, but they know to whom the Columbine students cried out as the bombs and bullets exploded. Their parents sang "love the one you're with," but today's youth gather at the pole and proclaim chastity until marriage.

The wake-up call that school killings have supposedly given our country isn't being heard by everyone, but it is resounding in the ears of our young. They are sick of being treated as the product of parents whose contraception failed and whose commitment to child-rearing is an occasional few seconds of conversation at random intervals. This generation is sick of being left alone in a virtual world where their gaming skills to kill as many as sadistically possible are their only measure of accomplishment in life.

Events don't lead to large numbers of lasting conversions. Christian experts on evangelism point out that fact. Whether they are Billy Graham crusades or terrible calamities, these occurrences seldom bring masses to a point of religious faith. Such circumstances may, for a time, encourage a revival of spiritual fervor. But such enthusiasm is generally short-lived.

Those who seek a restoration of America to a place of moral cognizance cannot depend on a catastrophe like

Columbine to provide the impetus. This disaster can be a building block to inspire a reconsideration of pious values, but any lasting return to true spirituality will require that each of us examine our own lives in the light of eternity. If Cassie and Rachel can help us do that, they will not have died in vain.

CHAPTER 2

COPYCAT CRIMES

Their names trip off our tongues. We speak of them in the same tone as earlier generations talked of Bonnie and Clyde or Jesse James. But these miscreants among us aren't hardened adult outlaws. In most cases their lives of crime have been limited to one day of dumbfounding brutality. We know them, not by the banks they robbed or the federal agents they eluded, but by the schools they attended and the cities they struck. Paducah, Jonesboro, Springfield, et al. And all but two of them are still alive, living reminders of the unimaginable dimensions of their deeds. In decades to come we will undoubtedly recall the anniversaries of their incidents, and we will probably still be wondering, Why?

Certainly this isn't the first time some demented mind has threatened the order of our civilization with some random act of insanity. Remember the 1982 scare of Tylenol bottles laced with poison? Have we forgotten the evil ingenuity that in 1993 planted syringes in Pepsi cans? What about those letters mailed indiscriminately, purveying deadly anthrax? And we can vaguely recall the several cases in which those afflicted with AIDS intentionally infected their victims with this slow death. Worse yet, we recollect that each of these events was followed by a copycat act(s) of equally malevolent indulgence.

Apparently similarly sick minds fixate on real or fictional models that generate public attention. When the movie *Money Train* came out, which had a scene of flammable liquid being squirted into a New York City token booth and set on fire, real-life robbers duplicated the act and badly burned a token clerk. After the 1984 showing of the TV movie *The Burning Bed,* in which Farrah Fawcett depicted a battered wife who set her ex-husband on fire, a viewer in Milwaukee poured gasoline on his wife and burned her to death.

Criminal science specialists call such acts "mode copying"—villainous minds looking for an archetype in order to successfully commit a crime. Some look for more than a competent way to circumvent the law. They seek significance and pursue a power trip to overcome their powerlessness. The key to the copycat is his or her feeling that there is nothing to lose.

COPYCAT KILLERS

Kids are copycats. One of the lessons learned from Littleton was that undue attention to such tragedies makes the next incident more likely to happen. In the days after the Columbine killings, black trench coats showed up throughout our country in places they hadn't been seen before. Violent graffiti suddenly appeared on bathroom walls. Anonymous calls threatened bomb scares, and Internet postings bragged of worse things to come. Some students even boasted of having explosives at home and tried to sneak weapons into schools.

"I can top that!" As absurd as it sounds, that's the attitude of some copycat kids. If Eric Harris and Dylan Klebold could kill thirteen, they can best that mark. As senseless as it sounds, anyone who doubts the capacity of kids to kill doesn't truly understand how near to the edge so many of our youth live. The child who feels alone and left out may want attention so badly that he will mimic a violent act. A moment-in-the-sun for a killing kid can mean national exposure—talk shows, morning newscasts, newspaper headlines, and magazine covers. It might not seem like a lofty goal to the average adult, but for an abused and emotionally abandoned youth, it looks better than the life he has now.

THE KILLINGS—WHERE, WHEN, WHO

A concise, orderly list of school shootings may allow us to grasp the chronology of the short history of this affliction and to have some sense about the revulsion we must feel, lest we forget and repeat the past.

Where: Moses Lake, Washington
When: 2 P.M., February 2, 1996
Who: Barry Loukaitis, age fourteen
What: .30-.30 rifle; attack on one classroom
Victims: One teacher and two students killed; one student wounded

Where: Bethel, Alaska
When: February 19, 1997
Who: Evan Ramsey, sixteen

What: Ramsey roamed the hallways with a shotgun and a paper bag full of shells firing until police captured him.
Victims: High school principal killed

Where: Pearl (Jackson), Mississippi
When: 8:10 A.M., October 1, 1997
Who: Luke Woodham, sixteen
What: .30-.30 rifle; fired during school opening
Victims: Two students killed; seven wounded; Woodham's mother stabbed before the school shooting

Where: Paducah, Kentucky
When: 7:30 A.M., December 1, 1997
Who: Michael Carneal, fourteen
What: .22-cal. Ruger pistol; used to shoot at students meeting for prayer before start of the school day
Victims: Three students killed; five wounded

Where: Jonesboro, Arkansas
When: 12:35 P.M., March 24, 1998
Who: Andrew Golden, eleven; Mitchell Johnson, thirteen
What: Three rifles and seven handguns; fire alarm pulled, forcing students outside, where gunmen were waiting on hill overlooking school grounds
Victims: One teacher and four students killed; ten wounded

Where: Edinboro, Pennsylvania
When: Friday P.M., April 24, 1998

Who: Andrew Wurst, fourteen
What: Opened fired at eighth-grade dance
Victims: One teacher killed; one teacher and two students wounded

Where: Springfield, Oregon
When: 8:00 A.M., May 21, 1998
Who: Kipland "Kip" Kinkle, fifteen
What: .22-cal. semiautomatic rifle and two pistols; indiscriminate shooting in school commons area
Victims: Two students killed; more than twenty wounded; parents killed before attack on school

Where: Richmond, Virginia
When: 9:55 A.M., June 15, 1998
Who: Unidentified fourteen-year-old freshman
What: .32-cal. Llama semi-automatic handgun fired
Victims: Teacher and school volunteer wounded

Where: Littleton (Denver), Colorado
When: 11:25 A.M., April 20, 1999
Who: Eric Harris, eighteen; Dylan Klebold, seventeen
What: Handgun, rifle, two shotguns and more than thirty pipe and propane bombs; massive attack through school building and bombs planted outside in cars and in various locations
Victims: One teacher and twelve students killed; twenty-three wounded

Where: Taber, Alberta, Canada
When: April 28, 1999
Who: Unidentified fourteen-year-old boy

25

What: Walked into school with .22-cal. rifle and shot two 17-year-old students
Victims: Local Anglican minister's son, Jason Lang, killed; one wounded

Where: Conyers (Atlanta), Georgia
When: 7:55 A.M., May 20, 1999
Who: Thomas J. Solomon, fifteen
What: .22-cal. rifle; shots fired as students assembled for class
Victims: Six students wounded

In addition to the eleven major school shootings listed above, there are six others that received less publicity, but resulted in eight dead and six wounded:

Where: Grayson, Kentucky
When: January 18, 1993
Victims: Two dead

Where: Amityville, New York
When: February 1, 1993
Victims: One dead and one wounded

Where: Redlands, California
When: October 23, 1995
Victims: One dead and one wounded

Where: Blackville, South Carolina
When: October 12, 1995
Victims: Two dead and one wounded

Where: Lynnville, Tennessee
When: November 15, 1995
Victims: Two dead and one wounded

Where: Stamps, Arkansas
When: December 15, 1997
Victims: Two wounded

Perhaps the most frightening aspect of these lesser-known incidents is this: The tragedy of school shootings has become so frequent and the carnage so severe that the six shootings outlined above have barely made a dent on the public's consciousness. Yet, the families of fourteen victims must face a lifetime of loss and suffering, which is no different from the families who suffer in better-known places such as Paducah.

THE COPYCATS

As shocking as the actual litany of evil compiled by those who actually pulled the triggers on classmates and teachers, is the long list of those who would have if they could have. In the month after the Columbine killings, there were many copycat attempts. Schools were closed in the District of Columbia and Independence, Missouri, as bomb-sniffing dogs searched campuses. In Wimberly, Texas, five fourteen-year-old boys were charged with plotting to blow up their junior high school. In Keystone Heights, Florida, police charged a fifteen-year-old boy with possession of a destructive device after they found homemade napalm in his bedroom. In Houma, Louisiana, a seventeen-year-old boy was charged with felony terrorizing after he donned a black trench coat at school and walked around pretending he had a gun.

Police in New York City arrested five thirteen-year-old boys who allegedly plotted to bomb their Brooklyn school. They were charged with conspiracy for drawing up a "hit list." In Bakersfield, California, officers arrested a thirteen-year-old boy at school who carried a loaded gun and a list of students and teachers who "deserved to die." Schools in Weyauwega, Wisconsin, were evacuated for two days after threatening notes were found. In Kalamath County, Oregon, sheriff's deputies checked area schools after written threats that students planned to bring stolen guns to school and start shooting. For a list of other copycat incidents, see page 181.

THE PSYCHOLOGICAL SIMILARITIES

The good news in this bad news is that teenagers aren't very inventive. They imitate behavior, especially bad behavior, and that trait gives us a warning of what to look for. The catch is knowing how to spot a troubled teen. Parents and leaders of youth must carefully study the warning signs of youthful rebellion and prepare for the worst. Every threat is a potential act, and anything a kid says about endangering the lives of others should never go unnoticed.

Though I have already listed pertinent information about these kid killers, I will repeat their deeds below, with special emphasis on the emotional and behavioral motivations behind their actions.

Barry Loukatis, the fourteen-year-old killer from Moses Lake, Washington, suffered from severe depression. He felt inferior to other students, and actually targeted and killed a jock who had teased him. The violence was probably

Loukatis's personal expression of the conflicts he felt at home. His mother was suicidal, and his parents' marriage was headed for divorce court.

Luke Woodham, the sixteen-year-old who fired on Pearl, Mississippi, students, had been abandoned by his father at eleven years of age. He was slightly overweight, and other students taunted him about his pudginess. They even suggested he was a homosexual. Insults seemed to rile him easily, and he displayed few coping skills. He killed his mother before turning his rage on his fellow students.

Michael Carneal, the fourteen-year-old from Paducah, Kentucky, who shot students attending a before-school prayer group, was also accused of being effeminate. Though both parents were at home, he suffered in the shadow of his exceptionally bright older sister. He was frequently depressed and displayed erratic, almost psychotic, paranoia. Such behavior allowed him to successfully cop a guilty-but-mentally-ill plea.

The two Jonesboro, Arkansas, child murderers—Andrew Golden, eleven, and Mitchell Johnson, thirteen—were clearly troubled. Though Golden was living with both of his parents, Mitchell's were divorced and he was bounced between them. Both Golden and Johnson displayed mean, bullying behavior. Both were rejected by girlfriends, and Johnson was teased for being fat. Those who knew them said the two were excessively aggressive around other students.

Kip Kinkle, age fifteen, first murdered his Springfield, Oregon, parents before wounding twenty students. His parents previously tried to help him, but he languished behind his popular older sister. Kinkle had taken Ritalin and then Prozac. He was a loner who had been expelled from school and was headed for a troubled-youth program.

Eric Harris, eighteen, and Dylan Klebold, seventeen, the Columbine killers, both came from two-parent families. Both were socially inept, Harris so much so that he took the antidepressant Luvox. The two were teased by jocks and called faggots. Klebold was especially shy and sad.

Thomas Solomon, fifteen, who wounded six in Conyers, Georgia, came from a broken home and was raised by a step-father. He was severely depressed and, like Kinkel, took Ritalin. A girlfriend had broken his heart, a point some students cited as a possible motive.

The characterizations aren't exact, but close enough. It doesn't take a semester in Psychology 101 to see the similarities. What we do know draws many convincing conclusions, and what we don't know would likely further confirm these findings. Of these nine young killers described above, four came from troubled homes. (And we have no way of knowing what went on behind the closed doors of the other five; some of those families may have been equally dysfunctional.)

One-third of the killers were taking prescription, mind-altering drugs, and more than half of them were recreational drug users. None excelled academically, none was popular in mainstream campus culture, and none had a circle of morally and socially stable friends. All were either without opposite-sex relationships or had suffered the indignity of female rejection. They were put down, put upon, teased, and bullied. Most importantly, there doesn't seem to be a single instance in which any of them was deeply spiritual, and none had parents who professed Christian faith as a dominant fact of family life.

In most cases, it was what these kid killers didn't have that characterizes them. They didn't have acceptance. They weren't well-liked, and no one seemed to sense their deep feeling of isolation and identity crisis. They weren't connected to other family or community members. Several had brushes with Christianity, but not one of them confessed an active participation in church life. Whatever else they didn't have, they didn't have a strong faith in God.

THE MARGINAL KID

Marginal. Jot that word down. It's one of the early warning signs you mustn't miss. When you spot a child who isn't connected to church, family, home, or classmates, look out. He or she may be looking for an exit from life that will guarantee infamy and notoriety. Think of it from this standpoint. A meaningless life of being ignored can be exchanged for a starring role in a Hollywood scriptwriter's plot. It's the shot at immortality that will make a seemingly worthless life have some sort of identity.

Luke Woodham said, "I killed because my whole life I felt outcast and alone." Andrew Golden, who joined Mitchell Johnson in the Jonesboro, Arkansas, killing spree, was raised by his grandparents while his parents worked. Mitchell never got over the loss of his father through his parents' divorce. As one murderer told psychiatrist James Gilligan of Harvard Medical School, "I'd rather be wanted for murder than not wanted at all."[1]

Today, the marginal kid isn't alone; there are other misfits to relate to on the Internet, where any kind of information about guns and bombs is freely available. Now, for the first time, every deviant on earth can link up with every other oddball and conspire to kill.

In the midst of the question "Why?" almost everyone

who wants to know why kids go wrong has missed asking the more important question—"Who?"

That answer is easy. The checklist of behaviors to watch for starts with a penchant for animal cruelty. Kip Kinkle, the Springfield, Oregon, killer, tortured cats and delighted in putting firecrackers in the mouths of squirrels.

A preference for violent movies is also high on the list. How many more times must we hear that the movie *Natural Born Killers* was one of the most-watched videos by school shooters before we say, "Duh, I guess brutality in art is imitated in life."

Bullying, threat-making, a history of abuse and neglect are also signs that a young life may quickly spin out of control and inflict more damage than anyone could imagine. All such behavior is probably a sign of alienation, which produces fear, anger, hopelessness, and frustration. If unresolved long enough, these emotions can become the paradigm for an act of tragic proportions.

If we've learned anything from the school shootings, it's that the marginal kid, the campus pariah, may be a ticking time bomb.

CREATING THE COPYCATS

"Violence begets violence."

"He who lives by the sword will die by the sword."

Those two maxims are not only spiritual laws that govern how we act individually, they are also corporate charters for the way we respond collectively to the violence that inundates our culture. For too long we have sent a green light to the troubled children in our midst that blood and gore isn't reprehensible. We've made a multimillionaire out of a Portland, Maine, writer whose homage to fear and terror has made him the biggest selling author of our time. To the psychologically troubled teenager who may already be predisposed to violent actions, we have given the outline to destructive behavior.

The nonstop saturation coverage of tragic events like school shootings has also become a kind of advertising. This seemingly endless stream of minute attention to every detail of how crime is committed is potent and persuasive. I live in Colorado, and I can tell you that every night of every year in recent memory the lead story of the nightly news on local affiliates is about that day's most gruesome murder. While we have the moviemakers under the microscope, why not turn the lens to the splatter stories that anchor local television coverage in almost every major city?

Advertising? That's exactly what it is. Create an image, evoke a desire, elicit a response. The method is simple. Billboards do it. Print ads do it. Newscasts do it. The more an image is presented, the more its significance is enlarged. If done enough times, it becomes inescapable, a fixture in our minds. Its permanent picture is with us.

What television news, together with entertainment, has created is yet another entertainment form to promulgate an antilife ethic. What's really so different about the fast-paced and slick production, complete with musical background, of the nightly newscast and its commercials? The casual observer scarcely notices the segue from one to the other. Violent death in a Bruce Willis movie isn't all that different from the anchorman's droning about murder in the city, with cutaways to the crime scene, which further glorifies such violence.

There is even a name for this murderous mimicry—the Werther effect. Sociologist Dr. David Phillips, of the University of California at San Diego, coined the name after documenting the influence of published accounts of suicide. The name Werther comes from a character in *The Sorrows of Young Werther*, by the great German author Johann von Goethe. The hero, Werther, kills himself over unrequited love. When published, the book's depiction of Werther led to a wave of suicides across Europe, causing the book to be banned. Some victims were actually found with the book open to the very page where the hero does the deed.[2]

Remember when grunge rocker Kurt Cobain committed suicide? At least a half dozen suicides were booked as imitations, some having declared their emulation in writing. Twenty years earlier the untimely death of Jim Morrison had the same result. Marilyn Monroe's suicide solicited an uncounted number of emulators. Today teens have a choice. Those who are already depressed may allow their impressionable minds to identify with the perpetrators of violence, even as the rest of us sympathize with the victims.

In Part Two we will look at some of the possible reasons kids are killing kids: violent video games, irresponsible media—from music lyrics to television and movies, the pervasiveness of death in our society, satanism in the schools, lax parenting, and some youths' need for revenge.

Yet one of the solutions to copycat crime is so simple. Newspaper and news magazines can cool the incessant front-page coverage. The *Chicago Sun-Times* adopted that policy with the Littleton shootings, even as Katie and Matt were earning *Today Show* kudos for their interminably "sensitive" on-site coverage. The editor-in-chief argued that reporting is as persuasive as editorials and advertising. Before one more child who is desperately seeking attention sees Littleton or its likeness as a way to instant fame, we can present the facts, but downplay the story. The media did it with Clinton's indiscretions, and they should have done it with Littleton.

Our society's ability to watch news as it happens has gone beyond our concern for the victims. We want cameras at the scene, close up, even if the killers inside the classroom are watching their own killing spree telecast. The question is whether our thirst for on-the-spot coverage is outweighed by making the real story worse by letting the whole world watch.

PART TWO

WHY KIDS
KILL KIDS

CHAPTER 3

THE BLAME GAME

oom. The game describes the world of killer wanna-bes. No plastic pistols and Roy Rogers badges for this new breed of potential murderers. They haven't been taught in the good guys-bad guys school of social vengeance. The kids who kill are the product of a culture that is obsessed with totally wasting anyone who gets in the way, an attitude epitomized in the games they play.

When it comes to video games, parents are up against the second most popular form of home entertainment after television. Surveys show that 90 percent of American households with children have rented or owned a video computer game. Worse yet, approximately one-third of the top 100 video-console games have some violent content. The most bloody rank among the most popular. These "first-person-shooter games," as they are known, allow impressionable children to destroy entire civilizations by playing God and obliterating anyone in their way. They have become a ludicrous way of filling the minds of our young with the idea of death without the reality of real blood and guts.

But don't tell that to the video-game business, an industry

that knows no shame. At the Electronic Entertainment Expo in Los Angeles, less than a month after the Columbine killings, the $6.3 billion enterprise hardly blushed. Forty-inch monitors displayed the carnage of the latest in the *Doom* family lineage, as combatants armed with Uzis blasted opponents into bloody oblivion. The rationale for the industry's lack of contrition was voiced by the keynote speaker, who said, "No one has shown any connection what-soever between these games and tragic incidents such as Littleton, or to youth violence in general. But countless stud-ies have shown a linkage of youth violence to factors such as poverty, lack of parental involvement, family violence, untreated mental illness, the proliferation of guns, and sub-stance abuse."[1]

Other Expo speakers repeated the party line with perfec-tion. Games don't kill. Real guns kill. So do a host of other social ills. Put the blame there, and then feel free to line up to watch the next death match on the convention floor. And guess which booths drew the most attention? Those offering the most blasting and blood. For those who really want it, game experts readily showed shoppers how to make the vio-lence less graphic. Most didn't want the service. Said a Sony spokesman for its video-game division, "Shooting is a part of video-game culture." Unfortunately, so are kids killing kids.

DEALING DEATH: HANDS-ON

Sooner or later I had to do it. I couldn't just write about it, I needed to experience it. In some small way, I had to get inside the bodies and minds of these kids who kill. If Harris, Klebold, Carneal, Golden, Johnson, and Solomon did it, so should I. I loaded *Doom* on my computer and proceeded.

Like most of you reading this book, I had never played a violent video game, so this was stepping into a whole new world. No, it was more like a whole new universe.

The product packaging was enough to chill my spine. "Thy Flesh Consumed," read the front of the box. "Let the obsession begin," read the instructions. The marketing come-ons on the back of the box were worse. *The Ultimate Doom* invited me to attain "levels of the most explosive, mutant-laden, blood-splattered battle ever!" *Doom II* told me I had to "descend into the stygian depths of Hell itself!" What awaited me there? "Nastier, deadlier demons," the advertising told me. The color pictures on the box titillated my imagination with images of demons that, it seemed to me, only a mind possessed by them could conjure. One clearly was the image featured on Columbine killer Eric Harris's Web site.

Okay, so *Doom* isn't the worst game I could have played. But then I couldn't stomach *Grand Theft Auto,* where I would be guided in detail on how to steal automobiles. (And don't forget the extra points garnered for cop-killing in this game.) I'd been warned about certain games promising "kill your friends guilt free" and "get in touch with your gun-toting, cold-blooded murdering side." *Doom* would have to do.

The *Doom* instruction manuals were filled with profanity and vivid descriptions of what I'd encounter. Demons whose mouths were "filled with half-chewed flesh," creatures that "have no pity, no mercy, take no quarter, and crave none." "To survive," I was instructed, all I needed was a "killer instinct."

So, on with the game. For the next few minutes, I was Eric Harris and Dylan Klebold. All that I was missing was the adaptation these kid killers had made to the games by modifying them into actual facsimiles of Columbine High School.

What struck me immediately was how quickly I got going. Within minutes of loading the software, I was firing away. It was challenging and mesmerizing—a virtual-reality world of mayhem and murder that tugged at the emotions and drew me in deeper. I could easily envision a kid needing to quit to do homework or something else, and finding it difficult to arrest the allure of going on with the game. I was oblivious to the passing of time. The craving set in. I'll beat this thing. Just a little closer. Pow! Got him! Next?

With every turn, down every hallway, I encountered new obstacles. Well-armed "former humans." No worry. The instructions assured me I'd get by them with "some lead upside their head." I blasted away as fast as I could. The first thing I noticed was how close I had to get to my victim. That was risky. I might get hit. On the screen before me was . . . me, an icon with a mirrored image of my video alter ego that looked determined when the battle quickened and bloody when I was hit. Taking "damage," it was called. That's when my video visage looked like, according to the instructions, "raw hamburger."

No raw meat for me, so I hit the control button to fire as fast as possible. Shotguns. Chain guns. Rocket launchers. Plasma rifles. What an arsenal. I needed it. Demons prowled. Specters attacked. Lost Souls lurked. Pain Elementals (a game-coined name) lurked everywhere. Hell Knights and Barons of Hell awaited. Worst of all, the dreaded Revenant (another game name) was ready, a resurrected demon that had been shot but brought back into action more evil than ever. "No rest for the wicked," the instructions reminded me.

The battle wasn't easy. No wonder kid killers spend so many hours playing these games. Even with my arsenal that included an ammo box, a rocket case, and shells galore, I kept getting hit. It wasn't always an enemy who got me. I kept forgetting about those pesky exploding barrels, filled with toxic waste that kept going kablooey. The catch was to get them before they got me. The instructions were clear: "It might take several bullets to set off a barrel." Of course my thoughts went directly to the scene described by Columbine students, when either Harris or Klebold fired at a propane bomb. No question in my mind. I was entering the world of their murderous tutor.

Just one difference. A big one. My game instructions assured me that even though I was in a death match, I could come back from the dead and restart again at another level. In fact, I could resurrect and move on to the Nightmare kill level. There, the demons I had already dispatched would respawn. The games even had a name for this revived existence: "Eternal Life After Death," a place where I could keep on killing as often as I liked. And that's the difference. For Harris and Klebold, the killing field of Columbine is gone. There's no rematch, no new level. The game is over.

HOW GAMES CONDITION KIDS TO KILL

Didn't we all play shoot-'em-up versions of cowboys and Indians in the backyard? What's the difference today? When is a game no longer just a game?

First of all, the psychology behind video games wasn't developed by the gaming industry. It was concocted by the military as a more efficient means of getting soldiers to kill despite natural inhibitions. After World War II the Pentagon became concerned that only 20 percent of soldiers sent into battle actually fired their weapons. By Vietnam, that rate had increased to 95 percent. The reason? Simulators were used to desensitize the soldiers so that shooting at humans was made to seem more "normal." Many now believe, and I am one of them, that video games are the equivalent of military simulators that teach youngsters to enjoy the experience of wasting away virtual-reality opponents.

Does this actually make a kid kill? Obviously not every kid who plays a video game becomes a killer. But then not everyone who drinks heavily becomes an alcoholic. A variety of dispositional and genetic, as well as social and cultural, factors are involved. But does any concerned adult really want a kid to be proficiently trained to kill without remorse and with reward? If such simulation has transformed the army, do we want to take the risk it could recast our kids?

Playing is the basis for learning new skills. It is where we discover how to manage relationships and develop physical coordination. New synapses in the brain are actually created to take over the new talent. What if that "talent" is the bloodthirsty decimation of everything in your way? And consider what psychologists call "overlearning." That's what a concert pianist does when he practices a difficult passage until he performs with a dexterity that requires no thinking about the individual notes being played. When that same dexterity is applied to the killing behavior prompted by a violent video game, the overlearning allows cold-blooded actions to be performed automatically. Is that why the witnesses of kid killers, especially those obsessed with video games, described a detached coolness to their actions?

For the sake of arguing with someone who defends first-person-shooter games, here is a list of what is truly dangerous about them:

1. The linking of high scores to killing encourages amoral behavior as a reward for skill.

2. Normal play teaches children to control their negative inclinations. Violent video games prime them for uncontrolled impulses.

3. Overcoming the natural resistance to killing is a dangerous mental pattern to establish.

4. In normal child's play, a game stops if someone is hurt. In shooter games in which two or more participate, you are taught to destroy your playing companion.

5. Bad behavior, which counters good judgment, is favored instead of reasoned responses and moral considerations.

IS KILLING CHEMICAL?

Born to be wild. It's said tongue in cheek. But born to kill? It sounds absurd, and as of yet it hasn't been used as a defense in criminal trial proceedings—just wait. The evidence is mounting, and there may be some reasons to believe that killing is in some part chemical. Studies are revealing that there are genuine physiological differences between the brains of normal people and those who kill.

Is some kind of internal curse at work? Is there a biological disposition to violence? Adrian Raine, psychologist at the University of Southern California, has led studies comparing the brains of forty-one murderers with those of forty-one nonviolent people matched by age and gender. He found that murderers have poorer functioning of the prefrontal cortex, the part of the brain that sits above the eyes, behind the forehead. That part of the brain controls regulating behavior, the part that puts limits on our impulses.[2]

"Behavior is the result of dialogue between your brain and your experiences," writes Debra Niehoff in *The Biology of Violence*. "Although people are born with some biological givens, the brain has many blank pages. From the first moments of childhood the brain acts as a historian, recording our experiences in the language of neurochemistry."[3]

What fascinates researchers like Raine is that many murderers don't have the usual social signs associated with violent crime—a history of child abuse, poverty, domestic violence, and broken homes. In addition, some people raised in unhealthy environments seem to survive, while others seem genetically predisposed toward brutal behavior. These facts led researchers to investigate whether excessive aggression might be linked to biology. Many scientists have now concluded that bad genes coupled with a violence-prone environment can turn a child into a killer.

In response to those who see the "chemistry kills" argument as the ultimate insanity defense, researchers now postulate a combination of the nature vs. nurture debate. Dr. Bruce Perry of Baylor College of Medicine points out that repeated stress, such as abuse, neglect, and terror may actually cause physical changes in the brain. He says that the young brain of a child is especially vulnerable to hurt during the first years of development. The incessant flow of stress chemicals resets the brain's fight-or-flight hormones, putting them on alert. The result is a child who exhibits impulsive aggression.[4]

Does that mean that how school shooters were raised may have pushed them over the brink? Biologist Michael Meaney of McGill University believes that when parental care is inadequate, the brain decides that the world is a hostile place and sets up the person to be defensive.[5] Thus, the mean-spiritedness that's part of adolescent taunting can make some children react more violently to humiliation. They also become desensitized to violence. Their stress hormones are like a keypad pushed so many times it quits working. They become antisocial and emotionally insensitive. They have little empathy to the world around them.

Researchers also believe that neglected children have an impaired brain cortex, the part that controls feelings of belonging. When parents fail to form supportive relationships with their children at an early age, their offspring may grow up with a biologically underdeveloped capacity to attach to others socially. They then seek out an ideology that fits their sense of believing they are ostracized, and gravitate to certain music and video games which reinforce that script.

BLAME IT ON THE GOTHS

Everything about them is black. Their hair, their clothes, their fingernails, even their lipstick. Black, black, black. So, it seems, is their attitude. Sullen, depressed, somber. When they have their pictures taken, they seldom smile. The setting is likely to be a graveyard, or some place similarly foreboding. Their music is brooding, full of despair and hopelessness. They are attracted to Anne Rice, Edgar Allan Poe, and romantic poets like Shelley and Byron.

Some among them say they are vampires. Others say they are simply the undead. They frighten any adult who comes near them. They are the Goths, raised on the music of Bauhaus, Joy Division, and Siouxsie and the Banshees. And some social critics are blaming them for causing the cultural climate that causes kids to kill.

Goths aren't as easy to identify as some journalists who covered the Littleton shootings assumed. They span many cultures, from America to Europe, and many ages, from teenagers to thirty-somethings. They have in common dark, flowing, flimsy clothing, heavy makeup, affected pale skin, and depressing music. Their flamboyant appearance belies what is basically an introverted culture. Though accusations of violence accompany the latest interest in Goths, the fact is most Goths are almost absurdly apathetic. The trench coats associated with the Columbine killers would be out of keeping for a true Goth; their uniforms are generally more elegant with an emphasis on finery, ruffled collars, cloaks, and capes.

The Goth designation is rooted in period literature from the last two centuries. Such writings, which often contain a medieval flavor, feature allusions to dark mysteries and the supernatural. But to understand the gospel of the Goths, one must look deeper at the sense of disenfranchisement that propels some of the brightest and best of our youth to opt out of mainstream society and adopt the accoutrements of darkness and depression.

Those who associated Goths with shooters Eric Harris and Dylan Klebold were missing the mark. They and their friends, the trench-coat mafia, may have partially adopted the Goth look, but their beliefs were far from Gothic. Most Goths may look weird, but they are usually harmless, at least as far as violence is concerned. Goths think a lot about death and the beauty of the macabre, but their dark fantasies don't normally include racism, Nazism, and murder.

Music holds the Goth culture together. Their style grew out of the post-punk scene in Britain in the 1970s and the "death rock" of the early 1980s. The words are incantations, and the music is not necessarily loud like heavy metal but is incessant, almost hypnotic, electronic percussion.

Joy Division, one of the premier Goth groups, named after Nazi-era concentration camp brothels, established a fanatical cult following in the late 1970s. The Manchester, England, band of morose-minded members played dirgelike music accompanied with lyrical visions of gloom. Their performance career was short-lived; in 1980, Ian Curtis, their lead singer, committed suicide. At age twenty-three, he hung himself before the band was scheduled to start their first American tour. His lyrics expressed his view of life: "We knocked on the doors of hell's darker chambers/Pushed to the limits we dragged ourselves in."

Bauhaus, a British Goth-punk band, also now defunct, picked up on the popularity of Joy Division. Their equally disturbing songs are typical of the Gothic emphasis on the darker side of life: "Burn without pain . . . There is no choice/To counteract a threatening hand."

More sinister was the group Christian Death, which adopted a virulent, antireligious stance. Valor, the lead singer, summed up the band's philosophy in the song "I Hate You," which repeated the sentiment "I hate you" over and over.

The Gothic Girls, an all-male British band, helped introduce the Gothic image with their appearance of all-black leather. Their songs focused on futility and the devil.

A more popular band, The Cure, sported all-black hair and red lipstick, which contrasted with their pale faces. They called their music "mope rock," named for their moody, depressing songs ("I'm running out of time . . . if only I could fill my heart with love"). Lead singer Robert Smith helped them sell millions of records, more than most Goth groups.

The Sisters of Mercy featured lead singer Andrew Eldritch who made a Goth hit of the song "Black Planet" ("It's a black planet/Black world/Black, black planet"). Eldritch told his fans that beauty exists in horror and emphasized this philosophy with his deep baritone voice.

Other groups identified with the Goth movement include Skinny Puppy, Dead Can Dance, The Mission, The Cult, All About Eve, and Fields of Nephilim. Few new bands arrive on the scene, and the music of Goth remains rooted in groups like those above, who collect their royalties in absentia. However, for those insisting on new Goth music, there is Switchblade Symphony, Coil, Haujob, Wumpscutt, Mentalo, the Fixers, and the French band Die Form.

Why do kids go Goth? For some it is the music. For most it's the sense of community, a feeling of belonging with other outcasts who are equally misfitted for mainstream society. Goth culture also gives a sense of power to kids who feel alienated. By differentiating themselves from "normal" society, they feel strength in their dissension, much like the hippies of the 1960s. Consequently, Goths often attract the sexually confused, such as homosexuals, lesbians, and transsexuals.

Goths also contain a significant number of those interested in vampirism and witchcraft. Since satanists dress similarly, the link seems apparent. Actually, Goths are more into paganism, white Wicca, and earth magic than black magic.

On the positive side, Goths are often bright and intellectually inclined youth who are attracted by the Gothic acceptance of anyone who doesn't fit in anywhere else. They are more inclined toward poetry and art, rather than violent computer games and celebrating Hitler's birthday. The most harm they portend is toward themselves.

In the words of a countercultural pastor who ministers to the Goth culture, "Goths take their stress and pain out on themselves as cutters, piercers, slicers, suicide addicts. They will beat themselves up in their guilt and their sorrow to prove how real their pain is. They are some of the most creative, interesting, wonderful gifted people I have ever met, and some of the most troubled."[6]

Now that the Goth scene has been outed by the press, what's next? Perhaps nothing. Maybe Goth itself will go mainstream. Chances are, the real Goths will go underground, and true Gothic believers will become more extreme in their fascination with all things dark and deathly.

CHAPTER 4

MEDIA-MADE MURDERERS

I've got my lunchbox and I'm armed real well, Next M——gonna get my metal, Pow pow pow!" These words from Marilyn Manson's song "Lunchbox" are the litany of the next kid killer. Though Manson argues the tune was really about his bashing kids on the playground with his KISS lunchbox, that argument seems somewhat disingenuous and self-serving. The lyrics could be construed as an invitation to commit murder concealed in a musical formula.

Manson, whose real name is Brian Warner, at one time attended a private Christian school. His response was to rebel. He now says, "I wanted to do everything that I wasn't supposed to do. I went to heavy metal and satanism and the occult . . . I identified with the villain—the fallen angel. I never wanted to be like Jesus; I wanted to be like Lucifer."[1]

To emphasize the outlaw attitude of his band, each member assumed a name featuring a first name of a well-known woman, and a second name taken from a famous serial killer. Thus, the other band members are: Daisy Berkowitz, Twiggy Ramirez, Madonna Wayne Gacy, and Sara Lee Lucas.

Before Marilyn Manson's platinum-selling stardom

brought pressure from his record company to cool his miscreant mannerisms, he openly bragged about his affiliation with the Church of Satan. While Manson excoriated Christian critics as exaggerating his excesses, he made no bones about his devotion to the teachings of the late Anton LaVey and his commitment to the me-first ethic of misanthropy.

Ironically, Manson's manifesto of satanism appeared in the same issue of *The Black Flame* (publication of The Church of Satan, Volume 6, Numbers 1 & 2) that featured an article about my confrontation with leaders of the late Anton LaVey's diabolical organization. Elsewhere in the magazine, an interview with Manson focused on his hateful attitude toward Christians and his adulation of LaVey. Manson made no bones about his unadulterated commitment to the Church's philosophy of animalistic behavior based on survivalistic Darwinism. His mannerisms and music, according to Manson, were a deliberate philosophical extension of his satanic beliefs. Manson admitted he grew up reading the writings of famed black magician Aleister Crowley and Anton LaVey. "Satanism seemed right to me," he said. He thanked LaVey for "his inspiration" and then explained how he uses the teachings of the Church of Satan in his music.

For Manson's fans who argue that his lyrics have nothing to do with diabolical indoctrination, Manson declared, "I incorporate satanic philosophy, more times subtly than others. It gets across the philosophy without the name 'satanism.' After people get close to me, I let them know of my affiliation with the Church (of Satan)."

In the article, Manson took things a step further. Apparently, his songs aren't his only vehicle for the forces of darkness; he seems to view his concerts as an actual focus of demonic energy. "The concert is satanic. Just by being in the audience, you are entering my own personal satanic ritual."

Lest anyone think he is just an entertainer with benign feelings about Christians, Manson dispelled all doubts. He declared that he would "like to destroy Christianity" but considered Christianity a necessity to remind people of Satan's existence. "I find positive things out of negativity," he concluded.

After reading the above, should anyone be surprised that most of the school shooters have been Marilyn Manson fans? Their feelings of anger and rebellion were fueled by Manson's music. In addition, according to Manson, by merely being around his music they were inducted into an atmosphere of the demonic.

Social and spiritual anarchism has been the underlying philosophy of every school shooter. Where did they get this idea? Manson, who would now like to be excused of any accountability for the toll of bloodshed in Littleton, Colorado, declared months before the first shot was fired, "I take the role of the Anti-Christ . . . I will scare America, and rightfully so."[2] Sadly, that demonic evangelism has borne fruit, as those kid killers who claim Manson as their hero have upped the body count in our classroom corridors.

In the weeks following the Columbine killings, Manson maintained relative silence. A number of his concerts were cancelled, and those surrounding him ducked for cover. When Manson did go public about accusations that he was at fault, he struck back by attacking Christianity.

In a *Rolling Stone* article entitled "Columbine: whose fault is it?" he argued, "Christianity has given us an image of death and sexuality that we have based our culture around. A half-naked dead man hangs in homes and around our necks . . . Is it a symbol of hope or hopelessness?" With blasphemous intensity, Manson declared that the death of Jesus Christ was "the most famous murder-suicide" and "also the birth of the death icon . . ."[3]

While Manson argued that media coverage of such events as Columbine is regrettable, he absolved his own music, which features perverse portrayals of sexuality and satanism.

He concluded, "The devil we blame our atrocities on is really just each one of us."[4]

DOES LIFE IMITATE ART?

Can a song kill? Do the words, the content, the meaning of any expression in art or drama influence conduct?

The idea that the media creates a social atmosphere in which horrors like Littleton are possible isn't new. Back in 1972 the Surgeon General's office produced a report on "The Impact of Televised Violence," warning families about the causal link between television and the conduct of children. In 1976 the American Medical Association's House of Delegates passed a resolution that stated, "The House declares TV violence threatens the health and welfare of young Americans."[5]

Was the movie *The Basketball Diaries* responsible for the Moses Lake murders and the crimes of Michael Carneal? In the film *Heathers*, featuring Christian Slater, the actor dons a black trench coat to get even with the school's cool clique. He evens rigs the gym bleachers with explosives. Were the Littleton killers copycatting?

What is media violence, anyway? It's more than a body

count. Yes, the average child is bombarded by thousands of violent acts, but what context is ascribed to these nefarious deeds? Take Leonardo DiCaprio's character, for example. In *The Basketball Diaries* the outrageous antisocial violence of the antihero killing classmates was gratuitous, a response to social humiliation that several kid killers have copied.

A starting point might be to teach children the difference between aggressive acts of unjustified hostility and legitimate images of morally acceptable ferocity. When Christ took a whip and drove the moneychangers from the temple, the zeal of God consumed Him. The same can't be said for the movie *The Matrix*, which features a final shooting scene so intense, it would be humanly impossible for any person to fire so many rounds so savagely at so many targets. Likewise, the depictions of brutality in *Pulp Fiction* and *Natural Born Killers* promote violence. Yes, even the Bible has violent scenes, but there is spiritual depth and meaning in the context of the ferocity. And Scripture never condones violence for the sake of violence.

Adults need to understand that the violent influences in our society are only partial causes for kids killing kids. While the media may be blamed for having fueled the fire of their indignation, it wasn't the sole source of these kids' anger. What made them want to get even was a deeper spiritual vexation that was unnoticed by those who could have stopped it. Instead, they seized upon the obvious causes.

Even President Clinton was forced to inject the bully pulpit of the White House into the debate after Littleton. Though he had been previously chastised for taking huge sums of political money from Hollywood entertainment moguls, apparently the influence of focus groups convinced Clinton that he had to at least appear to be concerned. The result was a presidential directive to the Federal Trade Commission to investigate whether the entertainment industry deliberately markets violent material, which is rated for adults, to children. "Our children are being fed a dependable daily dose of violence, and it sells," he declared.[6]

Clinton borrowed the idea from Senator Sam Brownback (R-Kansas), who had proposed the same idea two weeks earlier in an amendment to a juvenile justice bill approved by a Senate vote of 98 to 0. Clinton's proposed study was granted only $1 million dollars and was projected to take up to eighteen months to complete. Do we really need taxpayers' dollars to tell us what most Americans with common sense have already concluded?

Here's how our culture works. The same television networks that tout multimillion dollar Super Bowl spots to advertisers cringe at the suggestion that anything they portray on the screen could make anyone do anything. Are they pocketing advertising dollars under false pretenses, or hiding behind a specious argument that no progenitor of art can ever be held accountable if life imitates it?

In the aftermath of the Columbine killings, the networks ran for cover from the hailstorm of public criticism. Even the distributor of "Jerry Springer" promised no more daytime talk salted with profanity, violence, and physical confrontation. The WB Network momentarily cancelled two episodes of "Buffy, the Vampire Slayer," the teenage melodrama about vampires, including one that showed a wicked high school principal transforming into a sixty-foot snake. The "Buffy" students were destined to slay the serpent until network execs decided the story line was too close for comfort. They finally aired it more than two months after Littleton.

Television programmers adamantly insist that television

violence does not contribute to actual violence, but they backpedal in fear of viewer backlash and political intrusion. For example, in the days after Littleton, Leslie Moonves, president of CBS Television, declared that the networks did not "bear responsibility for what happened in Littleton." At the same time he rejected a pilot about Mafia families because of gun violence.[7]

A recent meeting of Hollywood screenwriters billed its gathering as an effort to discuss the topic "Guns Don't Kill People . . . Writers Do." While the topic's title was tongue in cheek, at least one veteran writer declared at the gathering, "We who create entertainment must honestly acknowledge and urgently address the responsibility we all have to eliminate excessive or gratuitous or unpunished violence. Otherwise, children will continue to kill children."[8]

In the wake of President Clinton's call for an investigation into media violence, Jack Valenti, head of the Motion Picture Association of America, said, "The reality is there are going to be subpoenas. You prepare for it by getting your lawyers all organized."[9]

There you have it. Hollywood's answer is to circle the wagons and call in the attorneys. And, oh yes, blame it on the guns. The logic of the movie industry is that people don't kill, guns do. By shifting the focus from human responsibility to an inanimate, cold piece of steel, their conscience is off the hook.

What the gun control advocates of Hollywood (many of whom hire expensive armed security agents to bodyguard their own families) forget is that to fire a gun, a finger must pull the trigger. And that finger is linked to a mind which is being criminally manipulated at the box office by ratcheting up the violent content of the latest film releases.

The screenwriter of *Die Hard* and *Die Hard 2*, Steven De Souza said, "Every picture I have done has come out more violent than what I wrote. I have sat at the screening of one of my movies and been stunned at the level of mayhem that somebody put on the screen."[10]

A proponent of the gun control's lobby, Rosie O'Donnell, badgered Tom Selleck on her TV talk show, demonstrating her bias against Selleck's appearance in an NRA ad. She conveniently forgot that in the Pearl, Mississippi, shooting, Assistant Principal Joel Myrick saved the lives of countless students when he used his own firearm to subdue the gunman, Luke Woodham. Myrick surprised the assailant, who had undoubtedly expected everyone to be unarmed. Consistently, the media finds it easier to blame anything rather than be accountable for its own indiscretions.

Perhaps those who grant slack to the media by suggesting its depiction of violence is cathartic or artistic haven't really looked much at violence in some of the more popular movies, which are at the top of our cultural index. Setting aside *Natural Born Killers*, and just considering movies from *Indiana Jones* to *The Untouchables*, children are accustomed to seeing heads severed by sabers, bullets tearing through flesh in slow motion, and blood spurting from disassembled appendages. The message is easy to understand: killing is glorious (it's those like Indiana Jones and Jean-Claude Van Damme who get the girls), violence can be used for humor, and the man willing to pull the trigger holds the power and makes the rules. As a culture we give lip service to the memory of Mother Teresa, but our fashionable images are those of the psychopath.

Is the media's influence obvious and direct? Certainly

not. But it does engender a cultural milieu that slowly cultivates a desensitized acceptance of violence. Life is seen as more threatening than it is, and real atrocities are viewed as natural and inevitable. The moviemakers have learned that this requires them to constantly increase the dosage of violent fare.

Teachers and students paid such little attention to the so-called trench-coat mafia. The notion that a group of misfits who talked darkly about bombs, worshipped Hitler, sketched pictures of demons, and spewed racial hatred wasn't considered dangerous is disturbing. The Columbine students I talked to immediately after the massacre seemed to have previously shrugged off the seriousness of such a cabal. Are we that jaded as a society, so inundated with the bizarre and the titillating, that we can't see the enemy among us because he looks so much like us?

The multibillion dollar media conglomerates continue to insist there is no evidence to prove a causal relationship between fictional violence and real kid killers. They hide behind this reasoning because they are technically correct; no one sees a movie and goes out into the night seconds later and commits mayhem. But just because the subtle causal relationship isn't documentable doesn't mean it doesn't exist.

Many studies show prolonged, continued exposure to media violence makes children more prone to commit acts of violence and approve of violent solutions to conflict. One well-known study conducted by Brandon Centerwall shows the connection between the initial introduction of television into a society and a sharply rising homicide rate thereafter. This connection has proven true in different decades and even vastly different cultures.[11]

Only the most profane and indifferent—and greedy—among us can continue to argue that life in modern society doesn't imitate art. We have the body count in the classroom corridors and a long litany of school shootings to prove it. What we lack is the will as a people to loudly declare that any parent who lets their child view violent movies and play violent video games is committing child abuse.

CHAPTER 5

PAYING FOR PADUCAH

In 1941, the country was in the midst of a debate about whether to enter a war. The attack on Pearl Harbor ended that debate. A similar cold-blooded attack, forever to be known as Littleton, has become the Pearl Harbor of America's cultural war.[1]

I didn't write those words. I wish I had. Jack Thompson, a Miami-area lawyer, did. Unlike politicians who check focus groups to determine which way the breeze is blowing in the culture war, Thompson creates his own tornado. And this time he is bearing down on twenty-five of the top entertainment conglomerates in America. His fury comes from the parents of Paducah.

In 1992, Thompson denounced rapper Ice-T's song "Cop Killer" at the Time Warner shareholders' meeting. He declared, "If Time Warner and the rest of the entertainment industry does not stop dumping its corrosive, harmful entertainment into the American culture, then eventually the parents of children harmed by that will successfully turn around and sue for damages."

The hall erupted into laughter. But as Thompson confirmed on my nationally syndicated radio talk show, "They aren't laughing now."

At the request of three sets of Paducah, Kentucky, parents who lost three daughters to the bullets of school shooter Michael Carneal, Thompson (along with his cocounsel, Kentucky attorney Mike Breen) has filed a multimillion dollar lawsuit. Targets of the suit include two Internet pornography sites, the producers of several computer games, and the makers and distributors of the film *The Basketball Diaries*.

The suit alleges that when Michael Carneal fired upon the praying students at West Paducah High School on December 1, 1997, his violent behavior was inspired by the entertainment industry. To defray critics, Thompson quickly points out he's not an ambulance chaser. The suit was filed four months after Paducah, just one week before the April 20 shooting at Columbine High School.

A few days after the Littleton tragedy, I invited Thompson to be a guest on my nationally syndicated radio program. My normal aversion to overly-litigious attorneys looking for a quick buck faded fast. I found Thompson forthright and intensely committed to making the media accountable for the bloodshed of our children.

He began by defining the legal precedent justifying his suit. "In March of this year," Thompson explained, "the United States Supreme Court entered a ruling that allowed to proceed a copycat violence case brought by a quadriplegic harmed by two teenagers who went on a rampage after they saw the movie *Natural Born Killers*. In fact, after the screening of the movie, the director, Oliver Stone, proclaimed to the adoring media, 'This movie is great. It makes you want to go out and kill somebody.'"

Thompson quickly got to one of his key points: *The Basketball Diaries*. The movie has been implicated in the shootings at several schools, including Moses Lake, Washington, and Paducah, Kentucky. I already knew that. What I didn't know was that the oft-cited scene in which DiCaprio, wearing a trench coat, sprays his classmates with gunfire was not in the original book from which the movie was adapted. In fact, Thompson said that when the book's author joined him for a *Today Show* appearance, he complained that his book had been altered.

Thompson accused the director of the movie of having admitted the scene was added to appeal to youth interested in violence. Thompson quoted the director as saying, "If we had made it true to the book, the kids wouldn't have come to see it."

"What an admission!" Thompson declared. "This was an R-rated movie that by definition can't be shown to children. And yet they targeted the movie to children and marketed it to them. That shows what a scam Hollywood's movie-rating system is."

Thompson added another criticism of *The Basketball Diaries*. "The head of New Line Cinema, who made this movie, said in the aftermath of the Littleton shootings, that his movie may have caused the carnage at Littleton and Paducah." Thompson claimed the producer said, "It could be that our movie was the final moment of dark inspiration, the last straw that caused the crimes."

"But what about the responsibility of parents?" I asked. "The entertainment industry is always hiding behind that argument. They say it's not their obligation to control what children watch—that's what parents are supposed to do."

Thompson was ready for that one. "Okay," he said, "let's talk about the parents of those three precious young girls that Michael Carneal shot. Those parents raised their daughters right. If they hadn't, they'd be alive today. They raised their kids to be in school and to be in a Bible study. That's where they were when they were shot. They died because they were Christians kneeling in prayer!"

Thompson went on. "It was the parents of Michael Carneal, the fourteen-year-old murderer, who dropped the ball. They let him spend countless hours on the Internet consuming antiwoman pornography. It's no coincidence that he shot and killed girls. Carneal's parents allowed him at the age of fourteen to watch the R-rated movie *The Basketball Diaries*. And Michael Carneal's parents, like millions of other parents, foolishly and negligently allowed him to play point-and-shoot video games that give the techniques to kill and the appetite to kill."

WHAT TEACHES KIDS HOW TO KILL?

His message is compelling, despite what anyone may feel about Thompson's lawsuit. Christian parents who did the right thing had been victimized by indulgent parents who did the wrong thing, and someone had to pay for it.

After a quick commercial break, I got back to the discussion. This time Thompson turned his attention to first-person-shooter video games, such as *Doom*. The attorney set out his proposition clearly.

"Michael Carneal walked into his high school having

never shot a handgun before in his life," Thompson explained. "Yet, he opened fire on a scrambling Bible study group, discharged eight rounds from a .22 semiautomatic revolver, and all eight shots hit their targets. Five were head shots; three were upper torso shots. It makes what Lee Harvey Oswald did from the Texas Book Depository in Dallas pale by comparison."

I was too shocked to let Thompson go on. I had to make sure I was hearing him correctly. "Hang on," I interrupted. "Let me get this straight. Are you saying that Michael Carneal had never fired a handgun?"

"Never!"

"Then are you alleging that Carneal learned the motor coordination skills to aim and successfully hit a target with a pistol as a result of a video game?"

"Yes," Thompson confirmed. "There's more. He used a firing technique that is totally counter-intuitive, or unnatural. He discharged one round at one target and moved instantly to the next one. In most cases, he aimed for the head. Then he discharged another round and moved to the next victim. This is a rapid-fire technique that's totally abnormal. Experts tell us the natural thing to do, especially for someone who has never fired a handgun, is to unload your weapon into a target until it falls and hits the ground. Where did Michael Carneal learn the methodology to shoot the way he did? He learned it from point-and-shoot, first-person, violent video games in which you're given a short amount of time to discharge your weapon, and you get rewarded for firing only one shot at one target."

Thompson continued to give his reasoning for why Carneal killed as he did. Though the subject of using video simulators as a means of training soldiers has been covered elsewhere in this book, Thompson's application to the Carneal case is enlightening.

"The military found in World War II, that the willingness of soldiers to discharge their weapons in a combat situation was very low because of the God-given instinct not to kill one's own species. The military has had to try, through operant conditioning, to overwhelm and suppress the instinct not to kill by creating a disconnect between the physical act of pulling the trigger with the awful cognitive realization that a life might end.

"How have they done that? The military uses video games, even taking the game *Doom* and modifying it to a military application. Bob, with video games, the willingness-to-kill rate is about 95 percent." Thompson made an important distinction. "In a military setting, soldiers are always overseen by an officer who questions the decision to shoot and the ethics of shooting certain targets. No such oversight is found in a video arcade, where you're rewarded for head shots. You see the brain matter splatter on the screen, and you are given the thrill of killing with no consequences."

I stepped in to raise an issue I knew my listeners were pondering. "My audience and I may agree with you," I insisted. "But aren't there First Amendment issues? How can you legally hold a video-game manufacturer responsible for someone who uses his recreational product as a means of learning to kill efficiently?"

"'Freedom is moving easy in harness,'" the lawyer answered, quoting Carl Sandberg. "Marketing a murder simulator, and that's what some of these video games are, isn't free speech. That's akin to saying a lawn mower makes noise, so it is First Amendment communication. A killing video game is an appliance, and the president should direct the Product Safety Commission to recall every first-person-shooter game that's on the market!"

COMMENTS FROM TWO CALLERS

My radio show was almost over, so I turned to the phone lines, even though I could have continued talking to Thompson, I was so fascinated by his assertions. I punched in line number four, and glanced at my video screen: Dan, age thirty-six, Phoenix.

"Dan, what's on your mind?" I asked.

The caller went directly to his point. "I think we should take responsibility for our own actions and not blame video games."

Immediately Thompson jumped into the conversation. "Let me address that. The Paducah parents worked extremely hard to get Michael Carneal put away for twenty-five years. The reason they did is because Michael Carneal is fully, morally, criminally culpable for what he did. But let's be consistent. Let's talk about responsibility for other people. What about the people who make violent video games? They probably send their kids to private schools and try to keep them away from the influences they are more than happy to sell to other kids. Are they at least not financially responsible for having targeted other people's kids?"

"Dan, don't you feel that Hollywood and video-game producers bear some responsibility?" I asked. "Do you want to let them off the hook completely?"

Thompson added his viewpoint. "How about a drug

dealer who sells drugs to somebody else's kids? Is he responsible, or do we just blame the kid when he dies?"

"Well, we blame the kid who took the drugs," Dan said.

Thompson disagreed. "The law says differently. The higher you are in the distribution chain, the more culpable you are. I think Americans have figured out that Hollywood can't violate the golden rule. You can't do to other people's children what you won't do to your own and get away with it."

I felt it was time to bring Dan's reasoning closer to home. "Dan, do you have children?"

"Yes, I do. I have three of them. And they play games like *Doom,* and none of them are killers. It all comes down to the parents."

"What movies would you let them see?" I inquired further. "Would you let them go see *The Basketball Diaries* and *Natural Born Killers?*"

"Sure. Yes. As long as you're responsible parents . . ."

I couldn't let that statement pass unchallenged. "Dan, you're not responsible by definition. You don't even know what's right and what's wrong! How old are your kids?"

"Eighteen, fourteen, and seven."

"What video games do they have?"

"*Mortal Kombat* and . . . "

Thompson interrupted. "That figured in the Conyers, Georgia, shooting," Thompson chimed in.

"How's a video game the cause of somebody getting shot?" Dan demanded.

"The Conyers, Georgia, shooter, T. J. Solomon, had a skill that he wouldn't have had before the video game," Thompson explained. "There's no way to explain how Solomon and Carneal used a totally unnatural firing technique, other than by the games they played."

It was my turn to try and set the caller straight. "It's obvious to me, Dan, that you don't draw any ideological connections between people's actions and what influenced those actions. But somehow your children knew enough about these video games to want them. How did they know these games existed?

"They saw an advertisement. That's how they were lured into getting those games. The advertisement alerted you to the potential of purchasing those games. That in itself proves there's a connection between the message given to your mind and your actions, which result from that message. Can't you see that, Dan?"

"Yeah, but I've never gone out and killed anybody."

"No, but you called this show because you know that ideas have consequences, and you wanted to express your opinion," I argued. "Dan, as a parent you'd better think about your seven-year-old learning that it's fun to blow somebody's head off!"

By now I was completely exasperated with Dan. I asked him one last question. "Is there anything you won't let you kids do?"

I was surprised by his contradictory answer. "I won't let them listen to certain kinds of music because it's profane."

"Wait a minute," I said in response. "Let me see if I've got this straight. You won't let them listen to profane music, but you will let them play profane video games."

I didn't wait for Dan to respond. I was so frustrated by his argumentative comebacks, I decided he'd taken up enough of the program. But if I thought Dan's comments illustrated irresponsibility toward our children, the next caller, a Texas substitute teacher named Jeanie, told about the actions of a public school teacher, which stunned me even more.

Jeanie explained how she had subbed for an advanced computer class for three days. On the second day she noticed that the students were playing video games after they finished their assignments.

"Was this in the school, on school equipment, and on school time?" I wanted to know.

"Yes," Jeanie answered. "But what really concerned me was the game they were playing—*Doom*. Then they showed me another game called *Quake*. I found out that because this was an advanced class, it had two periods a day. So they were in that class for three hours. A lot of them chose not to go to lunch and instead stayed in the room and played these games. That's all they did for more than three hours a day."

I asked how these students got the games.

"The students told me that the video-game company rep came and left them," Jeanie said. "That upset me, so I decided to look more closely at the software boxes the games came in. They actually had violence and profanity warnings. The students told me that the regular teacher gave them permission to play the games without any restrictions."

Just when I thought Jeanie's story was bad enough, it got worse. She explained that she found *Doom* video-game posters and T-shirts in the supply room. The purpose? When the students reached a new level by the efficiency of bloodshed, they were rewarded with these items, which had also been left by the game company.

I thanked Jeanie for her valuable information and went back to Thompson. His advice for parents was critical.

"We need parents to check out their own school systems and find out if these games are being played in the same way Jeanie described," the lawyer advised. "And don't be surprised if you don't get cooperation from the school administration. To acknowledge these games are being played on school time and on school premises is to admit that school officials are being negligent, that they have allowed toxic substances, just like drugs, in the hands of our children."

A FINAL WRAP-UP

I thanked Thompson for joining me on the show, and turned my attention to the audience and delivered my editorial.

"Parents, we're fighting a holy war with Hollywood. We're facing an enemy that has taken control of many of our school systems." I leaned closer to the microphone and spoke with all the conviction I could muster. "People like Dan, and that teacher for whom Jeanie subbed, have put an entire generation at risk. Evil people have targeted the minds of our children for greedy gain. They have put our offspring in harm's way. As never before, we must be diligent to watch over the lives of our children, and pray."

I signed off, took off my headphones, and leaned back in my chair. As a parent, the broadcast had touched me emotionally and stirred me to pursue the care of our kids with even more diligence. It had saddened me to think that such innocent lives could be so callously disregarded by self-centered parents and teachers.

As I wrapped up the paperwork finalizing the day's broadcast and prepared to leave the studio, I was reminded of what Vice President Al Gore said during the Columbine memorial service on the Sunday following the tragedy: "I don't know why human beings do evil."

Whether Jack Thompson and the parents he represents are justified in pursuing their legal course of action is for the courts to decide. I, for one, wish him well. What I do know is that I've had enough of the "oh-what-do-we-do?" syndrome.

Sorry, Mr. Vice President, if you don't know "Why?" I do. Human beings are evil because they still perpetrate Eden's rebellion. They are evil because they choose to continue Lucifer's insurgency against God, and because those in authority, such as parents, educators, politicians, and some preachers, don't dare declare, "All have sinned and fallen short of the glory of God!"

The writer of the movie *L.A. Confidential* and the ultra-violent film *Payback* claimed that, when it comes to media violence, determining what is morally acceptable "is only for me to answer in my mind."[2] That reaction to school shooting violence is so intolerable that it demands its own "payback." Somebody will have to pay for Paducah—and Littleton—and all the others. If those who unscrupulously use the media don't pay with their pocketbooks, our children will pay with their lives.

CHAPTER 6

KIDS AND THE CULTURE OF DEATH

A lot of students say things like that." That's the way a friend of the Conyers, Georgia, shooter, T. J. Solomon, described the would-be killer's comment about wanting to kill himself, just before he fired on fellow students. The friend didn't take the portent seriously.

Not take it seriously? A fifteen-year-old somberly speaks of taking his own life, and no one pays attention? A lot of kids talk like that?

Yes, they do, and as a cultural whole, we're not paying much attention. When it comes to life-and-death issues, we provide no clergy to commiserate, let alone a psychologist with a trained ear to hear the despair. In most states, the public schools are lucky to have one mental health professional for every one thousand students.

Could it be that we don't want to listen? Sure, we're too busy, but even when we're not, are we really listening? Studies tell us that parents today spend 40 percent less time with their kids than thirty years ago.[1] I wonder if the parents of the teen who wrote these words knew he was thinking of death: "I long to blow up and shoot everything I can. What I don't like I waste. Feel no remorse, no sense of shame . . . I don't care if I live or die."

Those words were on the Web site of Littleton shooter Eric Harris.[2] Dylan Klebold once wrote about Satan opening a day-care center in hell. Harris and Klebold both collaborated on a video for a class project in which they dressed in trench coats, carried guns, and blew away jocks.

A few weeks after Littleton, I had dinner with General Colin Powell. With the days of the Gulf War and his role as National Security Advisor behind him, General Powell today works with at-risk youth in a program called America's Promise: The Alliance for Youth. But at heart he's still a soldier, this time fighting the enemies of injustice, illiteracy, and poverty.

I recalled that General Powell was present the day of the Columbine memorial, and asked him why he thought Harris and Klebold did what they did. I wanted a soldier's perspective, the insights of a man accustomed to being in harm's way, a man who understood what makes a man kill.

General Powell leaned back in his chair and paused to summon the full impact of his more than three decades of soldiering. He looked as serious as I could imagine him being on the battlefield. "Bob," he said, "I'm not sure whether those kids went in there to kill or to commit suicide."

It was an answer I hadn't expected. But reflecting on the information above, perhaps he was right.

I can envision Harris and Klebold, carnage all around them, the acrid smell of smoke filling their nostrils, the shriek of fire alarms silencing their thoughts, proudly smiling at each other. They had accomplished what they set out to do: to destroy their lives in such a severe way that they would forever be remembered for the sheer magnitude of their mission. With self-destruction could come immortality, the ultimate power trip for these powerless adolescents.

KIDS AND THE CULTURE OF DEATH

As we search for an answer to why it all happened, perhaps we miss the point. In the end Harris and Klebold may have successfully fulfilled their mission, as General Powell suggested. They must have known that there was no reasonable way to exit alive from their rampage. The nihilistic nature of their actions, capped by their own senseless self-destruction, was the message: violence for violence's sake, killing for the sake of killing, and dying without purpose or meaning. Life, they said, was meaningless. Pointless.

Keep in mind that these were kids steeped in satanic philosophy, where man is but another animal, no more or less virtuous than a wild beast. They were schooled in Darwinism, where the gap between a cockroach and a human isn't measured by the soul, but by the passing of millennia. They read the writings of Ayn Rand, whose "objectivism" sees man as the master of his fate, a fate which could just as nobly choose death as life.

In this milieu death doesn't seem so somber. It's not just inevitable; it's almost "friendly"—certainly not to be feared. That's the twist the dark side of death makes on Christian logic. "Death, where is your sting?" the apostle Paul taunted life's last enemy (1 Corinthians 15:55). The question was rhetorical because of the resurrection.

For too many of today's youth, the sting of death has been removed, not by an overcoming Christ, but by an easy familiarity with the wasting of life. It's one thing to associate military service with death and stoicism in the face of human suffering. But our children are supposed to learn justice, compassion, and mercy. And we are supposed to be nurturing parents, not drill sergeants.

We have become a death culture, and our youth are being desensitized to killing and death because of it. The signs are all around us.

DEATH IN THE MOVIES

I've talked before about the influence of the media, but now I'd like to look briefly at movies and death. Do movies and the media portray our death culture to kids? I believe so.

In *The Rage: Carrie 2* (shown widely in theaters in the days just after Littleton), jocks viciously taunt outsiders until one girl kills herself by jumping off the high school roof. Another student wreaks revenge by using her telekinetic powers to pulverize other students. In *Payback,* Mel Gibson shoots his rival's face off and in turn gets his toes hammered.

Less than thirty days after Columbine, the written sequel to *Silence of the Lambs* hit the market, serving up the cannibal Hannibal Lecter, a man who snacks on his victim's internal organs. Somehow it seems less than entertaining to read the author's description of the sounds humans make when their ears are cut off, when our own ears can still hear the sounds of students, their hands over their heads, screaming as they ran from their high school library. The time has come to make gory and gratuitous death less popular and less profitable.

DEATH IN THE COURTS

As the national soul-searching continued after Littleton, a major court decision said more about why kids kill than did any of the network commentators. In Madison, Wisconsin, a state appeals court ruled that a woman who tried to kill her unborn child by drinking too much alcohol could not be charged with homicide. The reason? The court ruled that "we are persuaded that the term 'human being' was not intended to refer to an unborn child."[3]

This reversal of a prior circuit court ruling was the result of charges brought against this woman for attempted murder. The mother, who was worried about the child's race and the pain of childbirth, went on a drinking binge to end the pregnancy. She was quoted as saying, "I'm just going to keep drinking and drink myself to death, and I'm going to kill this *thing* (emphasis added) because I don't want it." She spent the day at the bar before giving birth.

The child was born with a high blood-alcohol level and suffered from a low birth weight and physical abnormalities. Prosecutors said that because the child was born with injuries that were the result of the mother's stated attempt to kill the fetus, they had no choice but to file the attempted murder charges.

The court's ruling that an unborn child is not human is an exacting extension of the original *Roe v. Wade* 1972 Supreme Court decision declaring that a fetus is not a person and has no right to life. As a consequence, any student today, knowing the easy access of abortion and hearing about the Wisconsin decision, could conclude rightly that human life—theirs and their potential murder victims—has no value.

As death has become so ordinary, life has become much less sacred. Consider the message the following outrage sends about the value of human life. As police and prosecutors struggled to deal with the Columbine, Port Huron, and Conyers cases, a congressional judiciary panel tried to reach a consensus on whether to make it a crime to transport another person's minor daughter across state lines to get the girl an abortion.

The same "abductor" considered under the possible legislation couldn't even legally take the pregnant girl across town to get a vaccination, let alone make it possible for her to undergo a medical procedure that is terminal for the unborn child and possibly life-threatening to the mother. That such an issue would be debatable is itself a sign of moral paucity. Yet, opponents of the legislation argued that it was a "thinly veiled attempt to chip away at a constitutionally protected right."[4] In light of such decisions, don't the courts bear some responsibility for kids killing kids?

Today's youth are bombarded with a steady diet of insensitivity toward human life. They see through the euphemisms "pro-choice," "a woman's right," and, in the case of assisted suicide, "death with dignity." All the lies of those who have no fundamental regard for life as created in God's image can't quell the soul's understanding that the cessation of life, for any cause, is murder.

America's current culture of death can also be seen on the faces and on the bodies of the youth who roam our malls and congregate in our classrooms.

DEATH IN OUR CHILDREN'S LIVES

"You can't judge a book by its cover." Agreed. But looks say a lot about the attitudes of the heart, and tattooed biceps, countless body piercings, electric green hair, and assorted T-shirts with unprintable profanities are the signs of spiritual dissolution. Across the country, social liberals are running to the defense of the different. Common sense may tell most of us that outer appearance may well speak of inner ideas, but that lesson is lost on those who still champion the "rights" of students, even if they want to wear black trench coats to the classroom.

As I read article after article in Denver-area newspapers in the days following the worst mass killing ever in an American school, one particular column caught my attention: the *Denver Post* article titled, "Unleashed torrent of hate leaves nothing but victims." The columnist reminded his readers that students of Columbine High had reported bathroom graffiti scratched on stall doors that said, "Satan will kill all jocks."

It seems that Satan intends to kill more than overly egotistical athletes. He is assaulting our entire culture, and he is succeeding. We live in a culture that is spiritually dead.

That deadness manifests itself in a generation addicted to drugs—and I'm not talking about the recreational kind. An estimated 500,000 to 1 million children and teens take prescriptions for antidepressants. Mental health professionals claim such intervention is necessary, since as many as one in twenty American preteens and adolescents suffer from clinical depression.[5]

Wait a minute! Before we shove more pills down the throats of our kids, shouldn't we ask some serious questions? Who has the right to say a kid is at such risk he must be medicated to the gills for his own benefit? What will such mind-bending do to a child who is taking chemicals designed for an adult brain? Are we steering an entire generation down a path that teaches them to escape the pain and conflict that builds character in favor of avoiding any angst that unsettles their emotions? Are we abandoning our relationship as nurturing parents and instead giving our children *drugs*?

An outward appearance of death, a fascination with death both spoken and written, and a reliance upon a drug-induced deathlike state—death surrounds our young people. Furthermore, kids even know how to build a bomb that they can execute themselves. The information is only a click away, on the Internet.

DO YOU WANT TO BUILD A BOMB?

It's so easy to make one. The instructions are clear and simple. Bombs are every school killer's dream weapon.

My dilemma is explaining how easy it is to follow these directions posted on the Internet without telling you exactly how to do it, for fear the wrong person will read this. The wrong person most likely already knows what I've just discovered, however. Just type "bombs" into an Internet search engine. Web sites list in detail what explosives and propellants to use, and where to get them.

Explicit instructions on how to get what you need suggest starting out in a gun store or a pharmacy. And if you can't get what you want legally, plenty of Web sites tell how to get bomb-building elements illegally. "If it becomes necessary to pick a lock to enter a lab, the world's most effective lock pick is dynamite, followed by a sledgehammer. There are, unfortunately, problems with noise and excess structural damage with these methods," one site cautions.

Can't find what you want in the pharmacy? Don't feel like breaking and entering? There's still hope at the local hardware store and supermarket. Ethyl alcohol and ammonia are easily accessible, nitric acid less so. Sulfuric acid? Right there under the hood of the car in a battery.

From there, with a few beakers, flasks, stirring rods, and

standard high school chemistry class equipment, you can be on your way to make nitroglycerine, TNT, or dynamite. These Web sites describe Molotov cocktails, chemical fire bottles, and bottled gas explosives.

At this point in my research, I encountered these words of advice to "terrorists and anarchists" in bold letters: "none of the ideas present here are ever to be carried out, either in part or in full. Doing so can lead to prosecution, fines, and imprisonment." Yeah, right. Is that why the next section vividly describes the use of ignition devices, including fuses, timers, and radio-controlled detonators?

I could only imagine the Columbine killers may have surfed the same territory I was logged on to. On his Web site, Eric Harris described a pipe bomb as "heart-pounding gut-wrenching brain-twitching ground-moving insanely cool."[6]

There it was in the next section that I searched on the Web: "The classic pipe bomb is the best known example of a metal-contained explosive." (Somewhere Harris and Klebold found they could do the job just as easily with a little PVC pipe, adding nails and broken glass to the mixture for maximum maiming.) Two pages and a link later I found: "Plastic piping can be bought at hardware or plumbing stores, and a device much like the one used for metal containers can be made. If the entire device is made out of plastic, it is not detectable by metal detectors."

Read enough? I presume you don't want to know all about lightbulb bombs, concealed book bombs (thick dictionaries work especially well), and even phone bombs (you answer, you're dead).

Who puts out this stuff? One site informed me that the anonymous evil genius behind such instructions attends a U.S. college and majors in engineering. Another site spokesperson claimed to head a crew called RSV (Random Senseless Violence). In addition to bombs, his regalia includes a crowbar, wire cutter, rifle ("leave small animals alone—use targets that deserve to be abused, like people"), and CO^2 cartridges (used along with a 32-ounce glass bottle of gravel for shrapnel).

By this time I've had enough. I sign off and go back to reality. I feel eerie. Dirty. I've been into and out of a world that feels evil. Extreme evil. What kind of mind would want to study all that stuff? What kind of mind would write it?

It's detailed, specific, and deadly. If cyberspace is inhabited by demons, they are concentrated in the bomb Web sites—murder in the making. Something inside me screams out, "It's got to be illegal!"

But it isn't. It's protected speech under the First Amendment. That's not all. When the FBI surfs Web sites like some of those I visited—literally hosted by terrorists—by law they are not allowed to save material from these sites on a regular basis unless they are conducting a criminal investigation!

According to the Bureau of Alcohol, Tobacco, and Firearms, federal agents investigating at least thirty bombings and four attempted bombings between 1985 and 1996 recovered bomb-making literature that the suspects had obtained from the Internet. That threat is many times greater today with the Internet's exponential increase.

In 1996, three junior high school students from Syracuse, New York, were charged with plotting to set off a homemade bomb in their school, based on plans they had found on the Internet.

With the constitutional issues involved, and politicians in general lacking the will to act on the matter, the Internet will likely continue to be a place of danger for children prone to violent impulses. What concerned parents have to keep in mind is that computer access without supervision can end up being a very "explosive" problem for the child who wants to know how to build a bomb.

As parents we need expectations that our kids will live successfully and do well. A young person in our culture should not ask the question of whether life is worth living. The matter of whether each person's place in the universe is valuable should never be questioned.

Life is sacred. Yours. Mine. And the lives of our children.

CHAPTER 7

SATANISM IN THE SCHOOLS

One element is common in many of the school shootings: satanism. You rarely hear much about this in the media or from educators or police. No one really wants to admit to this pervasive similarity, since that could raise difficult issues in court about religious freedom. Most prosecutors don't want to muddy the waters arguing about the separation of church and state. The humanistic approach of most criminal justice specialists makes them officially skeptical of anyone claiming satanic inspiration to commit a crime, and in other instances, police and prosecutors are just plain scared to confront the supernatural.

Four of the eleven major school shootings listed in this book were satanically motivated (Edinboro, Pearl, Paducah, Littleton). Of the other seven, three (Moses Lake, Springfield, Conyers) indicated strong demonic cultural influences. The others (Bethel, Jonesboro, Richmond, Taber) have not provided enough evidence to ascertain what forces precipitated the extreme evil.

1. EDINBORO, PENNSYLVANIA

He's not the best known of the school shooters—one teacher killed, one teacher and two students wounded—but Andrew Wurst is significant because he is part of the pattern of the occult connection in school shootings.

When Wurst walked into the eighth-grade dance at the middle-school prom in Edinboro that Friday night, April 24, 1998, no one could have suspected he would be a kid killer, though the warnings were there. Like the other school shooters, Wurst was a fan of Marilyn Manson. He had what other students described as a "sick sense of humor" and had warned he would "go to the dinner dance and kill some people."[1]

Wurst was so deeply troubled that he often talked about suicide, yet no one took him seriously. He nicknamed himself "Satan," but people thought that was for attention.

Yet Andrew Wurst was serious about suicide and satanism. So serious that he took his father's pistol and calmly walked into the school gym, hunted down John Gillette, a forty-eight-year-old science teacher against whom he had never expressed any grudge, and shot him on an outside patio. Then he walked back inside to the dance floor and methodically shot three more people.

2. PEARL, MISSISSIPPI

Most folks had never heard of Pearl, Mississippi, a small (population 22,000) blue-collar suburb of the state's capital, Jackson. But on the morning of October 1, 1997, a sixteen-year-old overweight sophomore with thick glasses named Luke Woodham shot it into national headlines. His eleven-minute rampage resulted in two student deaths, with seven others wounded.

At 7:55 A.M., Woodham, wearing a baggy overcoat, made his murderous foray into the school. He quickly headed toward the school's commons area where students congregated. Without pausing, he walked up to Christina Menefee, sixteen, whom he had dated a few times. (Christina broke off the relationship a year before, telling Woodham she wanted to see other boys.) Woodham pulled a hunting rifle from beneath his coat and fatally shot her in the neck.

He opened fire on others who fled screaming. Lydia Drew, age seventeen, was killed by a bullet in the back. Student Alan Westbrook tried to escape, tripped, and fell. A schoolmate remembers Woodham standing over Westbrook and cursing him for turning his back. Woodham coldly shot Westbrook with the deer rifle, missing his spine by less than an inch.

Investigators eventually learned that Woodham had acted in concert with six other Pearl-area teenagers who were part of a feverish plot to rid themselves of enemies. They took the name Kroth, culled from an obscure satanic reference in an Internet fantasy game called DragonSpawn. Wesley Brownell, seventeen; Donald Brooks II, seventeen; Delbert "Alan" Shaw, eighteen; and Justin Sledge, sixteen; were initially charged with conspiracy to commit murder. Lucas Thompson, sixteen, was arrested and held as a juvenile in connection with the killings.

The youths had apparently talked for a long time about a possible attack on the school. Police said the seven had adopted the motto, "We can't move forward until all our enemies are gone." They planned to cut the phone lines, set fires at the school using homemade napalm, and escape to Mexico with the intent of hiding out in Cuba.

Luke Woodham obeyed the orders of eighteen-year-old former Pearl student Grant Boyette, who referred to himself as "the father." Like Harris and Klebold, and most satanists, Boyette professed admiration for Adolf Hitler. Boyette proudly called himself a satanist and had been involved in serious black magic for five years or more. Ironically, his father and mother were founding members of a nearby Baptist church. Prior to his satanic involvement, Grant was known as a devout student who would say grace over his food in the school cafeteria. His Sunday school teacher said, "Grant accepted Jesus. I believe that he was saved."[2]

Grant Boyette and Justin Sledge, who appeared to be the ringleaders, had studied the writings of Friedrich Nietzsche, the nineteenth-century German philosopher. Nietzsche, who was also admired by Hitler, questioned the objectivity of moral evil, siding on the side of the gray as opposed to absolutes of right and wrong. (Satanists and those in black magic often read Nietzsche's writings because he dismissed the concept of absolute evil.)

Soon after Woodham's arrest, police discovered that Christina wasn't his first victim. He had murdered his mother, Mary, earlier that same day with a butcher knife. Police found out about this murder when they noticed a bandage on Woodham's hand shortly after his arrest. When policemen asked how Woodham cut it, he responded nonchalantly, "Killing my mom." The attending officer noted that Woodham did not seem at all troubled by what he had done.

Woodham stabbed his mother eighteen times. She was found dead with a blood-soaked pillow over her head, her arms slashed, apparently from trying to fight off her son. She had been beaten with a baseball bat. According to the coroner, she lived up to forty minutes after the attack, as her chest cavity filled with blood. What her son did as she died has never been revealed. Why he killed her is known. This profile of his motive bears witness to the abuse issues I describe in the next chapter, "The Road to Revenge."

Woodham testified that he really didn't want to kill his mother, and couldn't actually recall doing so. Woodham said that he tried to stop. "I just closed my eyes and fought with myself because I didn't want to do any of it," he said. "When I opened my eyes, my mother was lying in her bed dead. I wasn't in control of myself when I did that. I don't know if I killed my mother. I am sorry."[3]

Defense lawyers argued that Luke Woodham shouldn't be held responsible for his mother's death, but Luke explained otherwise. Here are his own words under oath: "I do love my mother. I just wanted her to understand. I remember I woke up that morning, and I'd seen red-eyed demons that I always saw when Grant (Boyette) told me to do something. They were telling me I was nothing. I would always be nothing, if I didn't get to the school, if I didn't kill those people."[4]

Whatever snapped inside Luke Woodham had passed the point of no return a few days earlier. The weekend before his mother's death, he said that for some reason he just stopped caring. Somewhere inside him a switch had been thrown, divorcing him from any emotional investment in the crimes he was about to commit.

Kids that I have counseled who are involved in satanism often describe a pattern of gradual desensitization that leads them deeper into devil worship. They do things that numb their feelings, such as destroying personal items that connect them to family and friends. Many practice cruelty to animals. Woodham did. So did Kip Kinkle, the Springfield, Oregon, killer.

To prepare for the school shooting, Woodham first killed his prize Shih Tzu puppy, Sparkle. With the help of Grant Boyette, he savagely beat the dog and then stuffed her in a plastic garbage bag. Of the incident, Woodham wrote, "I took the night stick and hit her in the shoulder, spine, and neck. I'll never forget the sound of her breaking under my might. I will never forget the howl she made. It sounded almost human. We laughed and hit her more." Then, he doused the sack with lighter fluid, set it on fire, and threw it into a pond. Woodham described the sight of the sinking bag as a thing of "true beauty."

At first the press acknowledged the satanic connection to the Pearl killings. Police admitted that they had found sacrificed animals and bonfire ashes in the woods where late-night occult rituals were performed. Murder was also on the minds of these occultists. Authorities say that Boyette plotted with Kroth member Donald Brooks II to smear poison on the doorknob of his house to kill Brooks's father. Another Kroth, Shaw, talked openly about how he loved the devil. He brought books on satanism to class to read to other students. Unfortunately, in today's youth culture, such antics are so common that no one took this seriously.

When Woodham finally went to trial in June of 1998, he took the witness stand against the will of his lawyers and testified freely. He began by proclaiming his love for the girl he had killed. He sobbed loudly and told the court he had felt like a "total reject" when she jilted him. Then he launched into an explanation of his satanic involvement, which, he said, resulted from his feeling like an outcast.

Woodham found a sense of belonging in the occult, which

drew him so deeply that he cast magic spells and worshiped demons. He was specific about what he had done, especially what his mentor, Boyette, told him: "You'll never amount to anything, unless you make a sacrifice . . . To give yourself powers, give yourself to the devil."

Boyette had described himself to Woodham as the "master of high demon activity." The relationship had started when Luke befriended Grant Boyette sometime in 1997. Boyette cast a spell from a satanic book on a teen. Later this teenager was run over by a car and killed, and Woodham believed it was the result of the spell. Boyette's control was complete. Boyette promised Woodham he could get his girlfriend Christina back, and that he could get even with his enemies through the occult.

"One second I was some kind of broken-hearted idiot and the next second I had power over many things," Woodham said, explaining how satanism gripped his life. "I went from failing ninth grade to a few months later reading books on astrophysics. It's the power Satan has given me."[5]

Woodham's lawyers argued he was insane. He said otherwise. In a police videotape made half an hour after he was captured, he professed his sanity. "I'm not insane, Sir," Woodham told authorities. "I knew what I was doing. I wanted to kill her. I got a gun. I ran inside the school. I ran up to Christina, and bam!"

In the confession, Woodham also told how he felt when he fired upon the other students. Of Lydia Dew, whom he shot next, Woodham said, "I shot her . . . I don't know why." He described the incident as follows: "It was like I was there, and I wasn't there."

Was Luke Woodham depicting the state of mental oblivion that a demon-possessed person enters? Scores of people who have experienced such states have related to me their feelings while under such evil control. They talk about being conscious, yet being out of consciousness. They may "see" and "hear" what they are doing, but it's as if someone else were doing it. Sean Sellers, a teen who was executed for his crime, vividly recounted to me how he performed a demonic ritual the night he murdered his parents. He remembered walking toward his parents' bedroom. The next thing he knew, he was standing over their dead bodies without any recollection of actually having pulled the trigger.

Years of experience in counseling hundreds of demonized people convinces me that Luke Woodham was in a demonic state when he opened fire indiscriminately. He probably shot Christina Menefee willfully, but that act gave permission for the demons he had previously conjured to take over and precipitate more mayhem.

Luke Woodham will never see the light of day. Upon his sentencing he admitted that he deserved the punishment meted out. He told Judge Samac Richardson, "I knew I was a sick and evil person. If there was a death penalty, I would deserve it."[6]

3. PADUCAH, KENTUCKY

On Friday, November 28, 1997, fourteen-year-old Michael Carneal warned his friend Ben Strong, a fellow student at Heath High School in West Paducah, Kentucky, "Stay away from Bible study. Something big is going to happen."

Strong paid little attention—he knew Carneal liked to pull pranks—but asked what was going to happen. Carneal wouldn't say. Strong joked that he would beat up Carneal if he tried anything. "You're not going to be able to beat me up after this," Carneal responded.

Over the weekend, Strong worried. The freshman, Carneal, had never shown any signs of violence. Strong was concerned the younger student might do something to hurt himself. He did not consider that Carneal might harm the Bible group that he led.

The next Monday morning, December 1, Carneal loitered in the hall. He watched and waited as the group of thirty-seven students met before classes began in their weekly prayer circle, which was held in the front lobby of the school. He waited for them to lift their bowed heads and say, "Amen." When they did, he calmly put in ear plugs, pulled a .22-caliber handgun out of his backpack, and fired more than a dozen rounds. He had four other guns and three spare clips of ammunition, all stolen from a neighbor. He shot three classmates to death and wounded five others. Killed were Kayce Steger, Jessica James, and Nicole Hadley, all three committed Christians.

As the students lay bleeding on the floor, Strong rushed to his classmate and told him to put down the weapon. Carneal did and begged for Strong to kill him. "I can't believe I'd do this," he said. Then he slumped against the wall, waiting for authorities. When they arrived, he broke down and cried and then apologized for what he'd done. Carneal was charged with three counts of murder, five counts of attempted murder, and one count of burglary for stealing the guns.

Bit by bit a profile of Carneal surfaced. He was an awkward freshman, quiet, with no interest in sports. He was a good student, receiving better than a "B" average. Along with his family, he attended St. Paul Lutheran Church, where his father was an elder. Psychiatrists reported that Carneal was tired of being teased. He confided that carrying a gun to school made him feel powerful.

As residents of McCraken County tried to figure out a motive, the truth gradually emerged. Though he never argued about religion with Strong, an outspoken born-again Christian, Carneal hung out with a group of vocal atheists who rebelled against the Bible-Belt mentality of the Paducah community. Together these outcasts delved into the occult. Carneal often stood watching the informal Bible study. Occasionally, he joined other rebellious students as they taunted the Christian group when they prayed.

Emulating satanists, this dissident group painted their fingernails black and dressed in black. Nevertheless, Carneal, the son of a prominent lawyer in the area, continued to wear wire-rimmed glasses and standard teen-issue blue jeans. He expressed his defiance in other ways—by often interrupting class and taunting authority figures with T-shirts emblazoned with defiant slogans.

In addition to his profile of occult inclinations, Carneal had similarities to other kid killers. Friends reported he spent hours playing violent video games. He also watched *The Basketball Diaries* and related to the scenes in the movie that ridicule religion. Carneal told investigators that the movie depicted what he did. He himself wondered if he got his ideas from it. (In the movie, the lead character experiences a narcotic-induced dream, strides into his school, pulls a shotgun from a black trench coat, and starts shooting.)

Two other aspects are significant to the spiritual implications of Carneal's actions. First, Carneal told a teacher that during the shooting he felt like he was out of his own consciousness, as if he were having a dream. Such disassociation is typical of those under demonic control. Second, prosecutors curiously noted that Carneal showed little emotion during the grueling interrogation and prosecution procedures. It was as if he hadn't shot those kids, and truly wasn't sure exactly how, or why, it happened.

At the time of his trial, Carneal entered a plea of guilty but mentally ill. He will spend at least two to five years in prison. His defense attorney, Chuck Granner, argued that because classmates had ridiculed the kid killer, he felt the shootings would bring him acceptance. The attorney characterized Carneal as paranoid with a schizophrenia-like personality disorder. "Michael understands that his feelings, attitudes, and beliefs at the time of the shootings were, in fact, wrong," Granner said. "He deeply regrets the overwhelming pain, the injuries, and the loss of life that his acts have caused."[7]

Carneal told his psychiatrists he was tired of being taunted and felt pressured by the accomplishments of an older sister, who became valedictorian of the school's 1998 graduating class. For those reasons he shot his fellow students?

There are unanswered questions. What about the occult connection and the satanic group? What about stories of animal sacrifices and other evidence of occult activity found in the surrounding area? Exactly what kind of personality disorder did Carneal have? If it was a Dissociative Identity Disorder (DID, also known as Multiple Personality Disorder, MPD), what about this disorder's connection to demonic possession? Did Carneal describe a "dream" of control by an evil spirit that entered him because of his anger and his interest in the demonic?

Ben Strong's father, a pastor at the Concord Assembly of God Church, said, "I believe there is a real demonic force that would drive someone to do this."[8]

Hoping to shed more light on the matter, I arranged to speak with Ben and his father on my nationally syndicated talk show. My staff dealt with their attorney, who was the spokesperson for the family. The Strongs insisted that the entire discussion had to be on a positive note about the healing God brought to Paducah as a result of the tragedy. I had no problem with giving adequate emphasis to that part of the story, but the Strongs refused to discuss any of the "sensationalistic" issues surrounding the shootings, including whether or not Michael Carneal was under demonic influence at the time. The attorney representing the Strongs explained that they were aware of my program's emphasis on spiritual warfare and did not want the interview to go in that direction. At the last minute, the attorney cancelled the interview.

I mention this incident to point out how hesitant both non-Christians and Christians are to deal with any satanic aspects of school shootings. I in no way want to impugn the integrity of Reverend Strong and his son. But their refusal to publicly confront the satanic aspects of this crime have left the nation wondering. It is my opinion that the failure of everyone concerned to address the spiritual implications of Carneal's possible satanic control has left a doorway open for the devil to continue inspiring other such crimes.

We may never know exactly why Carneal did what he did. The right questions may have never been asked, and a psychiatric diagnosis, underpinning the court's decision, has left any remedial efforts in the hands of state-appointed, secular mental health professionals. Whatever Strong meant by "demonic forces" will be left for eternity to reveal.

4. LITTLETON, COLORADO

In earlier sections of this book I reported on the involvement of Eric Harris and Dylan Klebold in witchcraft, vampirism, and the demonic images associated with video games. The first chapter detailed the witness of Cassie Bernall and Rachel Scott, both of whom died for their faith.

Two important questions must not be overlooked. Why were these two Christian teens singled out, and why were they specifically asked these questions? Did Harris and Klebold purposely hunt and stalk them because they were known to be Christians?

Perhaps the answer to the satanic link in the Columbine crimes comes from the fact that at least two other Christians were deliberately shot. With four guns, sixty-seven bombs, and two hearts filled with hate, the Columbine killers apparently didn't shoot all their victims at random.

Mark Taylor, sixteen, was a special education student who had transferred to Columbine just three weeks earlier. When the shooters started firing, he was witnessing to two Mormon classmates. An outspoken, born-again Christian, Taylor had just prepared to counter the Mormons, who argued that there are several ways to get to heaven. As he started to share his faith that Christ is the only Way—at that exact instant—a bullet ripped through his left thigh.

Taylor fell to the ground. Facedown, he lay unmoving, hoping he would go unnoticed. One of the killers shot him with four more bullets, including one that tore through his chest, collapsing a lung; this bullet miraculously missed his aorta by less than a penny's width. To say that Satan shot him is no stretch. To say that God spared his life is an absolute certainty.

In the library, the killers found kids huddled under tables.

A shotgun blast hit Val Schnurr, eighteen, and three other girls. Schnurr lay bleeding from nine bullet and shrapnel wounds. "Oh, my God," she mumbled.

The comment caught the attention of Eric Harris.

"Do you believe in God?" he demanded.

Schnurr had already heard what happened to Cassie Bernall when she confirmed her faith. Val could have kept silent. She didn't, and it nearly cost her life.

"Yes, my mom and dad brought me up that way," Schnurr replied.

Instantly, she fainted and fell to the floor. Somehow she was spared.

According to reports from students, Kacey Ruegsegger, seventeen, was shot in the face and shoulder after she also confirmed her faith.

Were these shootings of Christians just coincidences? If you think that, remember how Rachel Scott and Cassie Bernall were specifically asked about their faith in God. Consider how Taylor was stricken the moment of his Christian witness. Consider the following comments made by Harris and Klebold as they continued their slaughter. The savagery points to an inhuman compulsion to kill.

Lance Kirklin was one of the first shot, hit in his left foot, right leg, left knee, and chest. "Help!" he cried out.

"Sure, I'll help," he remembers a voice saying.

Kirklin looked up to see one of the shooters pointing a sawed-off shotgun at his face and pulling the trigger, blowing off the left side of his face.

Harris and Klebold celebrated with hollers and shouts of joy when someone was shot. "Peekaboo!" one of them said as he blasted a girl in the neck and face.

One student in the library recognized Klebold and called him by name. "What are you doing?" the student asked.

Klebold responded unruffled, "Oh, I'm killing people."

As smoke billowed, alarms blared, fire sprinklers sprayed, and strobe security lights pulsed, they walked about their killing field undisturbed by the suffering. When one of them momentarily ran out of ammo, he was heard saying, "Maybe we should start knifing people—that would be more fun."

The killers didn't just intend to blow up the whole place, they wanted to inflict the optimum pain when they did. A propane barbecue tank bomb near the cafeteria was wired to another gasoline tank that was surrounded with nails and BBs to maximize the destruction.

The savagery of it all. The calculated way it was carried out. The remorselessness and glee the killers expressed. It appears to have the touch of extreme evil.

It's no accident that kids in our schools today are involved in satanism. Unfortunately educators have forced Christians out, citing the separation of church and state. At the same time they have allowed satanists and other cult members into the schools.

WITCHCRAFT IN THE CLASSROOM

Sean Sellers, the celebrated teen murderer, was executed February 4, 1999, for the murder of a convenience store clerk. Sellers also killed his mother and stepfather while they slept, which he said was the result of a satanic ritual he had performed to call up demons. Sellers talked repeatedly with me, privately and over my nationally syndicated talk show. He shared how his involvement in satanism, which led to murder, started with the introduction of witchcraft in the public schools.

Seller's story is told in detail in my book *Larson's Book of Spiritual Warfare*, but I want to point out one aspect of his biography that is crucial to our understanding of why kids are killing kids in our schools.

Sellers began his journey into the occult, and eventually into full-blown satanism, when he attended a school-sponsored convocation where a witch was the speaker. The witch invited interested students to talk with her afterward, an overt attempt at evangelism. Sean responded, and, from that meeting, he developed an apprentice relationship with the witch that led him deeper into a study of the black arts.

Eventually Sellers read the *Necronomicon* and *The Satanic Bible*, incorporating such teachings into his understanding of witchcraft. He determined to break all of the Ten Commandments, a commitment which led to murder.

Sean Sellers would be alive today, and so would his three victims, if he hadn't heard that witch. The blood for these crimes is not only on Sellers's hands. The school officials who permitted the witch to speak to his school bear responsibility; their decision started the chain of events leading to Sellers's demonic activity. The same culpability lies at the doorstep of any person or parent who allows the continued intrusion of the occult into our schools, and this is much more prevalent than many parents realize. Two recent incidents indicate this activity.

SCHOOLS, SATANISM, AND THE LAW

Just months before the guns went off in Littleton, a seventeen-year-old witch attending Lincoln Park High School in suburban Detroit sued her school (with the assistance of the

American Civil Liberties Union) for refusing to let her wear a pentacle to promote her beliefs in witchcraft. (A pentacle is a witchcraft symbol, a five-pointed star, positioned with one point up and two points down, as compared to the satanic pentagram, which is reversed.)

The teenager, Crystal Sieferly, told a news conference, "Being forced to conceal one's religious symbol under their shirt is a form of shame." Her mother, who claimed to be a Christian, expressed full support for her daughter's efforts to embrace occultism.

The ban on such jewelry was part of an overall school policy, which forbade any student from sporting white supremacist and satanist accessories, as well as black nail polish and vampire-style makeup. According to the ACLU spokesperson, associating Wiccan (witchcraft) jewelry with satanists and racists "humiliated" the offended witch. Within days the school board, fearing an expensive legal battle, overturned its ban. The school even agreed to pay Seiferly's legal costs, at taxpayers' expense! The backdown came when a federal judge in Detroit ruled that the school's anti-pentacle policy violated the student's religious rights. As a result, both pentacles and pentagrams were okayed. The superintendent of Lincoln Park schools even apologetically declared, "I didn't realize that Wicca is a religion."[9]

Just one month after the Columbine killings, another victory for witchcraft was declared less than fifty miles away in Colorado Springs, Colorado. In this instance, eight sixth-grade girls were pulled from class when the vice principal discovered they were practicing witchcraft during school hours, and actually casting spells in the classroom. The students were caught reading a book called *Salem's Trials*—checked out of the school library!

The girls admitted they had recently watched the pro-witchcraft, PG-13 movie *The Craft*, about teenage witches. When school officials confronted the parents of the girls, they threatened to sue the school for interfering with the rights of their children to explore witchcraft and immediately contacted the ACLU for legal advice.

Several facts about these cases are particularly shocking. First, while the Bible as an expression of faith has been removed from the schools, witches and satanists can feel free to express their pagan allegiance with the full power of the courts behind them. Second, the parents in these instances were not worried that their children were involved in demonic practices. The Colorado Springs parents weren't even worried that these young teens had gotten their ideas from a PG-13 movie.

Such incidents should frighten any person of faith worried about where the next shots will be fired in a school classroom. The facts are simple. Jesus Christ is no longer welcome in our schools, but witchcraft and satanism are, with the legal sanction of the government. And the students who want to pursue the occult can't find a Bible in the school library, but they can find books on witchcraft.

It's about time that educators and the media admit what the devil is doing in our schools. So far only Christians seem to be willing to discuss the issue.

ADMITTING WHAT THE DEVIL IS DOING

A few weeks after the Littleton tragedy, Billy Graham held a crusade in Indianapolis, Indiana. In his first public statements following the shooting, Graham hit hard at the reality of demons at work in our world. In the past, Graham's ministry has tended to focus on positive issues of spiritual encouragement and not specifically deal with questions of evil, the devil, and demons. But the time had obviously come to be more direct.

"We have demons in our world," Graham told the audience of nearly 50,000. "We saw them at Columbine High School not long ago. And the Bible tells us that the devil is a thief and a robber who has come to kill and destroy."[10]

For his text, Graham chose the fifth chapter of Mark's gospel to tell the story of the demoniac in the country of the Gadarenes. He called the audience to prevail against the demons that work through bigotry, anger, sexual perversion, and lying. "But the devil is not going to win. Christ is going to win," Graham declared to thundering applause.

That didn't seem so possible at that time, however. In the aftermath of Littleton the suffering continued. Teenagers who should have been preparing for a summer of recreation and relaxation were nursing wounds and battling pain. Twenty-three students were healing—some in wheelchairs and hospital beds, some with bullets still in their bodies, and others with scars that would never go away. Still others were consulting with plastic surgeons, talking with counselors, and undergoing multiple operations.

Was Christ really going to win?

At least the tenor of the times had changed. Everyone seemed to sense that something desperately wicked "had this way come." A president mired in immorality talked about more carefully carding kids who try to see age-restricted movies. A vice president who would be president adopted a family-values campaign theme that sounded like former Vice President Dan Quayle's comment after that infamous Murphy Brown episode in which Murphy gave birth to an illegitimate child.

Even shock jock Howard Stern was admonished for stepping over the line in his comments about Columbine.

The face of religion in America soon turned from stained-glass windows to the spiritual legacy of teens carrying schoolbooks, martyrs for their faith. After Columbine, all around the city of Denver, teens were coming to Christ. Youth who were once awkward about discussing issues of faith were calling youth pastors and asking for help. Even a *Time* magazine columnist mused, "If we suspect that saints may sit beside us in the library and devils may drive BMWs and work in the pizza parlor and leave no telltale trail of ash as they go about their work, if we just find ourselves asking questions we haven't had occasion to ask before, we will know more than we did . . . and be wiser for it.[11]

For Harris and Klebold, one or two bombs wasn't enough, soon it was sixty-seven. Not just a couple of kids had been killed, now it was twelve. Even the most jaded secularist couldn't avoid reporting the immensity of what had happened, and how the kids who huddled in the cafeteria and choir room prayed—hard—because they meant it.

Suddenly the forces of evil were backing down. Denver-area newspapers started reporting on church meetings where kids who used to be concerned about good looks and fine clothes were asking deeply spiritual questions. A Marilyn Manson concert at nearby Red Rocks was cancelled. No kid who excused his Goth appearance and his satanic rock music was going to get anywhere with parents who used to say, "It's just a phase they're going through." Body piercing suddenly went out of fashion. Crosses on a hill overlooking the crime scene became the norm. Suddenly satanism didn't look so respectable to rebellious teenagers.

And parents like Darrell Scott, the father of Rachael Scott, began speaking out.

RACHEL SCOTT'S LEGACY

The quiet that filled room 2141 of the Rayburn House Office Building on Thursday, May 27, 1999, at 2:00 P.M., was powerful. On that day, at that time, Darrell Scott put the United States government on divine notice.

From the record of the United States House of Representatives, I quote the words of Scott in memory of his daughter:

Since the dawn of creation there has been both good and evil in the heart of men and women. We all contain the seeds of kindness or the seeds of violence.

The death of my wonderful daughter, Rachel Joy Scott, and the deaths of that heroic teacher and the other children who died, must not be in vain. Their blood cries out for answers.

The first recorded act of violence was when Cain slew his brother Abel out in the field. The villain was not the club he used. Neither was it the NCA, the National Club Association. The true killer was Cain, and the reason for the murder could only be found in Cain's heart.

In the days that followed the Columbine Tragedy, I was amazed at how quickly fingers began to be pointed at groups such as the NRA. I am not a member of the NRA. I am not a hunter. I do not even own a gun. I am not here to represent or defend the NRA because I don't believe that they are responsible for my daughter's death. Therefore I do not believe that they need to be defended. If

I believed they had anything to do with Rachel's murder, I would be their strongest opponent.

I am here today to declare that Columbine was not just a tragedy. It was a spiritual event that should be forcing us to look at where the real blame lies!

Much of that blame lies here in this room. Much of that blame lies behind the pointing fingers of the accusers themselves.

I wrote a poem just four nights ago that expresses my feelings best. This was written way before I knew I would be speaking here today.

> Your laws ignore our deepest needs.
> Your words are empty air.
> You've stripped away our heritage.
> You've outlawed simple prayer.
>
> Now gunshots fill our classrooms,
> And precious children die.
> You seek for answers everywhere.
> And ask the question "Why?"
>
> You regulate restrictive laws
> Through legislative creed,
> And yet you fail to understand
> That God is what we need!

Men and women are three-part beings. We all consist of body, soul, and spirit. When we refuse to acknowledge a third part of our makeup, we create a void that allows evil, prejudice, and hatred to rush in and wreak havoc.

Spiritual influences were present within our educational systems for most of our nation's history. Many of our major colleges began as theological seminaries. This is an historic fact. What has happened to us as a nation? We have refused to honor God, and in doing so, we open the doors to hatred and violence.

And when something as terrible as Columbine's tragedy occurs—politicians immediately look for a scape-goat such as the NRA. They immediately seek to pass more restrictive laws that continue to erode away our personal and private liberties.

We do not need more restrictive laws. Eric and Dylan would not have been stopped by metal detectors. No amount of gun laws can stop someone who spends months planning this type of massacre.

The real villain lies within our own hearts. Political posturing and restrictive legislation are not the answer. The young people of our nation hold the key. There is a spiritual awakening taking place that will not be squelched!

We do not need more religion. We do not need more gaudy television evangelists spewing out verbal religious garbage. We do not need more million-dollar church buildings built while people with basic needs are being ignored.

We need a change of heart and a humble acknowledgment that this nation was founded on the principle of simple trust in God. As my son Craig lay under that table in the school library and saw his two friends murdered before his very eyes, he did not hesitate to pray in school. I defy any law or politician to deny him that right.

I challenge every young person in America and around the world to realize that on April 20, 1999, at Columbine High School, prayer was brought back into our schools.

Do not let the many prayers offered by those students be in vain.

Dare to move into the new millennium with a sacred disregard for legislation that violates your conscience and denies your God-given right to communicate with him.

To those of you who would point your finger at the NRA, I give you a sincere challenge. Dare to examine your own heart before you cast the first stone. My daughter's death will not be in vain. The young people of this country will not allow that to happen.

On April 24, 1999, Rachel Joy Scott was laid to rest. It was a chilly, gray spring day filled with tears. More than two thousand people remembered this aspiring actress, pianist, and poet as a young woman who loved life and loved Jesus.

Rachel's white casket was adorned with one red rose. Her friends scrawled final wishes on the casket, using black markers. Her own mother inscribed, "Honey, you are everything a mother could ever ask the Lord for in a daughter. I love you so much. Mom."

One pastor who presided declared to the youth, "Pick up the torch that fell from Rachel's hand. It's up to you. Politicians and legislators have failed you. The police who couldn't keep you safe have failed you. And we your parents have failed you." When the pastor asked who was willing to heed his call, every young person in the building stood and raised an arm.

That's not exactly what Satan had in mind. It's more what Billy Graham suggested. No question about it. Satanism had held sway in the hallways of many schools in America. And the killers who embraced the ideology of extreme evil had frightened both their classmates and our culture. But this time the devil went too far. The truth was out. The Luke Woodhams would be taken more seriously next time. The Harrises and Klebolds would never again be able to say, "Heil, Hitler," without someone taking notice. If any good is to come out of Columbine, it will be because we, as a nation, have finally admitted to what the devil is doing, a perspective we must never lose if we are to keep our children safe.

CHAPTER 8

THE ROAD TO REVENGE

It will happen again. Someday, coming soon to a city near you, kid killers will spray yet another school with gunfire and senseless slaughter. There will be bodies and blood all over again. It will be so predictable and so preventable.

We'll know who did it. He'll be male, somewhere between fifteen to eighteen years of age, and he'll probably belong to a closed social circle of a few friends who share his penchant for outlaw music and bloody videos. There will be warning signs: pages of written omens displaying a fascination for violence, satanic doodles, flirtations with occult teachings, meanderings with satanic music.

The next kid killer will be angry and introverted, disenfranchised, and acting out a sense of powerlessness. He won't be a leader, a jock, a class president, or a student government candidate. He'll be an outsider who's anxious to get even. He won't be stupid. He'll have an above-average intelligence and an obsession with video games and computers.

His psychological profile will have been etched on our minds by the prior analyses of his prototype, the last time his kind pulled the trigger. We'll probably have done little to help people like him. Why? We're unwilling to admit what really caused him to do it. We won't have looked deep into our souls to see the spiritual slime that oozes across our land and engulfs our youth.

A PROPHECY TOO SOON FULFILLED

The words above that introduced this chapter were written just days after the Columbine killings. They were written *before* T. J. Solomon walked into Heritage High School in Conyers, Georgia, and shot six students, exactly one month after Columbine.

I wish my "prophecy" hadn't been fulfilled so soon. The fact that I could predict another tragedy so closely paralleling the Littleton incident didn't take any great powers of prognostication. And at the risk of sounding like a prophet, I repeat. It will happen again—soon, too soon.

The kid from Conyers wasn't a murderer. Though a practiced shooter, he aimed low. He could have used the high-caliber weapons he had access to in his stepfather's gun cabinet, yet he chose a low-powered .22 rifle. He didn't aim. He didn't chase people to gun them down, he fired from the hip with a pump-action sports gun.

Yet the lack of resolve displayed by T. J. was about the only thing out of profile. He was a loner, though he did go to church and he was a Boy Scout. He played the vicious video-game *Mortal Kombat*. T. J. wasn't a Goth and didn't idolize Marilyn Manson, but he was enamored with violent rap music, especially that of the late Tupac Shakur. In his bedroom police found printouts of bomb recipes and notes on where to plant explosives at his school as well as penned rantings about his despair.

What was most disturbing about Solomon wasn't what he did, but how a wearied public and his jaded fellow students responded to what he did. The real story wasn't about how shocked the suburban Atlanta citizens were, but how the incident was nonchalantly accepted as routine, expected, anticipated. It may be that since the Conyer's incident wasn't as bloody as the Littleton massacre, it was easier to accept. I suspect this nonchalance was because we thought of this as one of a series of incidents we had been through before and would go through again.

The scene was the same. Yellow police tape cordoning off the crime scene. Network TV trucks beaming the action to a watching world. Local anchors rushing to the scene, with makeup attendants standing by to carefully put every hair in place. Local affiliate helicopters buzzing overhead, capturing the action from a bird's-eye view. The vigil of parents waiting and wondering if their child had a bullet lodged in his or her body.

Journalists trotted out the usual adjectives: the shooter was "normal," the "last person" anyone suspected; he was angry; he had darkly suggested he might do something, and he had explored the Internet to learn what he might do with explosives.

It's as if every one of us is beginning to take these shootings for granted. The students I talk to have a grim resolve about their school being next on the list. They're not even sure what to do about the threats of violence that circulate. So what if some outcast kid says he may blow up the place? These high school students have grown numb, either because they see violence as inevitable or because they think, *If we deny the horror of this, we don't have to realize that it could happen here, in our school.*

115

THE DAYS OF OUR KIDS' LIVES

Should some of the blame for the condition of our kids be placed on the subculture of teenagers at school, at play, and in social situations?

Let's talk about numbers. We've all heard so much about the baby boomers that we may have overlooked the increasing numbers of children of post-boomer parents. A decade from now, the numbers of young people will be bigger than those of the boomers' generation. And the angst of their age will make the social climate of their era more volatile than any previous generation.

To consider what the next crop of kids will be like, look first at the teen-somethings today. They have been pampered and privileged. They haven't had to register for the draft. They've never known a recession. No known enemy has threatened their peace and security. They have been given greater access to more information than all prior generations of U.S. citizens combined.

Yet, in spite of all these advantages, some teenagers today tell me they feel neglected, alone, and emotionally abandoned. When I talk to them on my radio show or pray with them in person, I find that beneath their Hilfiger jackets and Abercrombie shirts, they are tortured souls, unable to relate to their parents. Their desperate need for attention causes them to cling to cliques. Some join gangs or develop antisocial groups that embrace racism and hatred. When I try to connect with these kids, they seem so immersed in their own world of computer games and television that their social skills of communication are almost nonexistent.

THE EYES HAVE IT

Everyone who has seen them kill, from Pearl to Paducah, from Jonesboro to Littleton, says the same thing: "Their eyes

116

seemed to show no remorse. They actually seemed to enjoy what they were doing."

A senior at Heritage High School in Conyers, Georgia, said of shooter T. J. Solomon, "He had that hate look." The senior was so startled, when she spotted Solomon carrying his rifle as he entered the school, that she disappeared into a phone stall and hid. She told a reporter later, "I knew that something really, really bad was going to start."[1]

How can our kids kill without conscience?

If you check out school killings across the country, you will find a consistency of emotional detachment. They killed without compassion, blindly following some inner impulse that became part of their very nature. It's as if the killers don't really comprehend what they're doing. Their familiarity with deadly violence is one of detachment, aloofness, total indifference.

These current kid killers aren't like the Henry Lee Lucases and the Ted Bundys of the past. Today's millennium murderers aren't adult malcontents; they're the kid next door, the waiter at the pizza place, the student in the computer class. They mask their rage cleverly. The tickers on their time bombs are set, but the fuse seems so far from being lit that they almost go unnoticed. But when they do kill, they display a ferociousness and yet a remarkable composure. They aren't just killing for a thrill—they are killing for revenge.

To understand the reason for such actions, we must first comprehend how such kid killers ever got on this road to retaliation. No one except the court-appointed mental health professionals has been able to interview the most prominent kid killers, but I don't have to talk to them personally to suspect the pattern in their past. What I will share in this portion of the book represents many years of counseling troubled youth and deciphering the spiritual principles behind their dysfunctional behavior. If we could get to the truth about what went on in the lives of the school shooters, we'd find the pattern was predictable.

THE THREE STEPS LEADING TO REVENGE

STEP ONE: ABUSE

The road to revenge starts when an impressionable child has been injured verbally, emotionally, physically, or sexually. Let me review how these four areas of injury affect a young person's emotional welfare.

Verbal Abuse

Remember the childhood dictum, "Sticks and stones may break my bones but names will never hurt me"? Don't believe it for a moment. The voice of a mother or father saying, "I wish I'd never had you!" or "You should never have been born!" or "Why did I ever bring you into this world?" is just as devastating as if the parent had struck the child with the back of his or her hand.

During the murder trial in which Luke Woodham received a life sentence for killing his mother, Woodham explained the rejection he felt. "She never loved me," he said as he wept on the witness stand. "She said I was the reason my father left. She said I wouldn't amount to anything. She told me I was fat, stupid, and lazy."[2]

This destruction of self-worth through verbal abuse— "You'll never amount to anything!" "You're no good!" "Look at you, you're worthless!"—may someday return in the form of catastrophic conduct, which is an attempt to disprove the parental allegation. After all, if a kid killer is on the cover of *Time* or *Newsweek*, doesn't that say something about his significance in the world? To the mind warped by verbal abuse, it does.

My experience while ministering in the realms of spiritual warfare has taught me that the effect of such harsh words can take place before the age when the child can speak, even prenatally. In fact, researchers now know that, behaviorally speaking, there's little difference between a newborn baby and a thirty-two-week-old fetus. The unborn baby reacts to loud noises, feels, and even dreams. The unborn baby distinguishes between the voice of Mom and that of a stranger, and responds to the reading of a familiar story. When observed on an ultrasound, the unborn baby reacts to its mother's laughter and moods. At some level, the fetus actually listens, learns, remembers, and behaves according to the level of comfort and assurance it receives. According to Janet DePietro, a Johns Hopkins University psychologist, "Behavior doesn't begin at birth. It begins before and develops in predictable ways."[3]

What's happening? Certainly the cerebral maturation process hasn't yet reached a stage where the unborn child can understand cognitively. I believe that the spirit of the fetus perceives the spiritual sense of what is being communicated. Remember, as an unborn child, John the Baptist was filled with the Holy Spirit when his mother, Elizabeth, heard Mary tell of the coming Christ child.

Emotional Abuse

Similar to verbal abuse, emotional offense occurs when feelings of rejection are communicated to a small child, even at a pre-perceptual age. Sometimes it isn't what parents do to an impressionable child, it's what they don't do. I've had kids say to me, "It's not as if Mom and Dad beat me or yelled at me. It's not that they consciously ran me down. They just weren't there when I needed them."

The most severe form of emotional abuse is neglect. A parent may be present in body without being present for the emotional needs of a child. At his trial Luke Woodham described how his mother often spent late nights away from home. He rarely saw his father, and no family relatives were ever close to him.[4]

Mitchell Johnson, the thirteen-year-old shooter in the Jonesboro, Arkansas, incident, was the product of a broken home where domestic life was marked by severe emotional abuse. An occasional visitor to the Johnson farmhouse declared, "There was dog crap on the kitchen floor, rotting food was lying on the counter for weeks. Little Mitch didn't look like someone I wanted my kid to play with. His clothes were dirty."[5]

There were other problems. Mitchell's father was arrested for stealing. His mother befriended a convicted felon and moved the man in her home as a live-in stepfather to the young boy. According to a sheriff's report, Mitchell admitted sexually touching the two-year-old granddaughter of his biological father's fiancé during a joint-custody summer vacation.[6]

Physical Abuse

While there is no direct evidence that confirms that any of the kid killers were victims of physical violence, I suspect that in one or more cases some mild form of abuse occurred. The remorselessness with which these boys acted out their vicious plans indicates an emotional detachment that often results from physical abuse. Killers like Loukaitis, Woodham,

Kinkle, Harris, Klebold, and others fired upon their victims with calm detachment. It's as if the people they were shooting weren't the real victims.

Were their fellow students substitute targets? Remember, Luke Woodham killed his mother before he shot eight others. Kip Kinkle killed both his parents before shooting two students and wounding twenty more. Perhaps these school killings were isolated acts, unaffected by anything the parents had done. I certainly don't wish to posthumously indict any of these parents and stain their memories for the family members who remain.

Yet, many times during my years of counseling disturbed teenagers, I have heard them say with resolution, "I'd kill my parents if I could get away with it!" Such bravado is often dismissed as an intemperate expression of adolescent rebelliousness. Yet sometimes, as I've heard young people say such things, I've looked deeply into their eyes and their souls, and seen that they really meant it. In almost every instance, that threat was made because of some form of physical violation.

Sexual Abuse

In my personal counseling experience, I encounter more youth with violent impulses as a result of sexual abuse than the other three forms of abuse combined. Nothing so devastates a person's soul and leaves him or her utterly vulnerable to the invasion of extreme evil, even demonic possession, as sexual abuse.

God has cloaked our sexuality with a sense of privacy and shame because it is the part of us that is most vulnerable. Our human sexual identity is the core of our personhood. Our maleness or our femaleness is the imprint of His creative impression upon our lives. If we are sexually blemished, all that God meant us to be can be confused. The litany of serial killers who were sexually abused as children—John Wayne Gacy, Henry Lee Lucas, Charles Manson, and more—bears witness to the fact that sexual violation can lead to the most callous of human crimes.

These notorious killers are representative of the general prison population. More than 36 percent of female inmates in state prisons and jails say they were abused sexually or physically by age seventeen. That is roughly twice the rate of child abuse reported by women overall, according to Justice Department figures. Counting physical and sexual abuse *at any age*, nearly half of all incarcerated women say they have been attacked, according to an article, "Prisoners Report Past Abuse," in *USA Today*. One third of all women in state prisons say they have been raped. The male prison population also reports the same rate of sexual abuse—double that of the overall male population.[7]

What this Justice Department information tells us is that those with violent criminal impulses are acting upon a self-image reinforced by the violence they have experienced. Those who are sexually abused come to believe they are bad and that bad behavior is expected of them.

Security expert Gavin de Becker, author of *Protecting the Gift: Keeping Children and Teenagers Safe*, believes the number one threat to children is adult sexual predators, and that much teenage violence stems from sexual abuse. He encourages parents to educate their children on how to thwart unwanted sexual advances. For example, children should be taught that their parents will always be receptive to hearing about any experience they've had, no matter how unpleasant it might have been. This breaks the conspiracy of silence often established by sexual violation and prevents a child from burying the incident, which may cause it to erupt in violent behavior later.[8]

I recall dealing with a nineteen-year-old young man named Brad who was headed for prison. He was handsome, talented, and well educated, but everything else about his life was in shambles. He was a repeat drug offender, an indulgence which had led him into criminal activity. His parents had brought him thousands of miles to meet with me, hoping that I could turn his life around. I spent a considerable time talking with Brad, but couldn't easily break through his emotional defenses.

"You do understand that your repeated brushes with the law have you headed for prison, don't you?" I asked.

Brad nodded. He showed no emotion and expressed no regret for his behavior.

"If you'll quit doing drugs, there's a chance your life can be salvaged," I encouraged him. "Show the court you want to make some changes, that you'll get involved in a rehab program and get out of the cycle of crime."

Brad responded coolly. "It's no use. You're wasting your time. I can't change, and I won't change."

"But, Brad, you've got everything else going for you. You were raised by fine Christian parents who love you and took you to church. You're a good-looking kid. And you're bright. Do you really want to spend the rest of your life behind bars?"

Brad shrugged his shoulders.

My experience in dealing with kids like this told me why he seemed so indifferent. "Someone, sometime, hurt you badly. Who was it?"

For a moment Brad seemed unconcerned. He looked

around the room and fidgeted with the arm of his chair. Then the apathy in his eyes turned to fire.

"If you really want to know, I was three years of age!" He paused for a moment. His body tensed. "It was the next-door neighbor. My parents let me go over there to play. At the time I didn't know what he was doing to me. How does a kid at three know he's being molested?" Brad turned cold again. "That's it. I don't want to talk about it any more!"

My heart went out to him. I wasn't surprised. I'd heard the same sort of story hundreds of times from hundreds of angry kids. Sometimes their parents didn't know what happened. Sometimes they didn't want to admit what happened. Sometimes the denial was so strong, even the young people had nearly forgotten the incident. But it came back, often in unconscious ways, to affect their behavior.

"Brad, you do drugs to run from what happened. But there's hope if you'll deal with the pain of the past. Face it. Acknowledge its horror. Admit how much it hurt. Forgive the man who abused you. Move on with your life so you can heal."

My pleading was in vain.

"I'm not going there," Brad said firmly. "It hurts too much, and I'd rather be behind bars than to ever feel again what that man did to me!"

In Brad's eyes I saw the same frosty detachment the student saw in the eyes of T. J. Solomon, the same expression that those who survived Littleton saw on the faces of Eric Harris and Dylan Klebold.

In most cases, we'll never know which of the schoolyard kid killers was abused, molested, or assaulted, or which of them hid in the darkness of the corridors of *Doom* to escape the pain of the past. We'll never know which one struck out at the students around him because he couldn't strike back at the one who misused him. Months after the Jonesboro, Arkansas, shootings, Mitchell Johnson admitted to having been molested. Was he the only honest one? Is that, in some cases, the missing "Why?"

I believe that killers like Harris and Klebold, who questioned their victims about whether they believed in God, must have been abused in some way that prevented them from perceiving the benevolent fatherhood of God. Psychological counselors know that our biological fathers play an important part in forming our image of God. When a father has not affirmed the identity of a child, any mention of, "Our Father which art in heaven," is met with belligerence and perhaps violence. That may be why they lashed out so savagely against any affirmation of faith.

If verbal, emotional, physical, or sexual abuse is not properly dealt with—if spiritual and psychological healing doesn't take place—the psyche develops what I call "spiritual scar tissue." Unless God intervenes, that person is destined for some inward self-destructive act or some outward expression of violence toward another person.

This abuse leads to the next step on the road to revenge: terror and trauma.

STEP TWO: TERROR AND TRAUMA

The abused youth I counsel express a sense of helplessness. "How could this have happened?" they ask me. Another common comment is, "It's not right, it's not fair!" In the case of sexual abuse, the victim usually says, "Daddies (mommies) don't do that. Men (women) shouldn't act like that. Daddies (mommies) are supposed to protect their children."

In the case of the most severe forms of abuse, that helplessness may be what psychologists call "learned." It is indoctrinated to the extent that an abuse victim may eventually submit willingly to continued abuse. He has "learned" that subjugation and humiliation is to be expected, and indeed welcomed, because it is supposedly deserved.

One of the most severe cases of adult traumatization I have encountered was that of a woman in her forties. In the midst of a prayer time during a spiritual warfare workshop I conducted, she suddenly started screaming, "This can't be happening. My daddy is a good daddy." The woman had spontaneously regressed to a repressed childhood identity, for whom the sexual abuse of incest was so real, it seemed to be happening at that moment. The task of healing her was accomplished after I convinced her childlike alter identity that, unfortunately, daddies are sometimes bad daddies. Then she acknowledged the victimization and admitted (though the sexual violation had occurred at age three) that the incest wasn't her fault. Once this woman recognized her false shame and guilt, the effect of her victimization was overcome.

Children who continue to act out the shaming of childhood violation often become invested with murderous passion. As I minister to them, they will sometimes react so vehemently they actually go through the motions of attacking their nonpresent perpetrator.

The abused person feels doomed for life. He or she may be bright enough to cope on a conscious level and survive socially, but inwardly the young person is looking for a moment when this terror can be released upon another. The young person isn't deliberately vindictive. He or she has merely started on the road to revenge and the process will play out unless intervention occurs.

A case I encountered in Canada illustrates this. As I was writing this section of the book, the front page of the Toronto *Globe and Mail* newspaper (June 17, 1999) carried the story of a seventeen-year-old boy, Adam Laboucan, described as the nation's most dangerous young offender. A ten-page psychological assessment had declared him virtually incurable. The latest of Adam's crimes was his confessed drowning of a three-year-old child. He had also pleaded guilty to a violent sexual assault on a three-month-old boy left in his care when he was fifteen.

The psychiatrist examining Adam discovered that a family friend had sexually abused him at the age of six. Adam first abused another at the age of ten when he sexually touched a cousin. Today Adam considers himself to be bisexual and admits to fantasies of having sex with children under the age of five. The government's court-appointed psychiatrist has diagnosed Adam as having "adjustment disorder."

My evaluation? Adam is a classic case of this process leading to revenge. Terrorized by what happened to him at a sexually formative age, Adam concluded that his lot in life was to do unto others what had been done to him. When the psychiatrist asked him about the murder of the three-year-old child, Adam responded, "I don't know why I did it."

None of the kid killers in the school shootings has any clear idea why he *really* committed the crime. Not one of them seemed to be coherent at the time. Yet, most adult criminals who act out an evil design have some sense of purpose; their logic may be convoluted, but they have a goal, such as killing for money or unrequited love. The schoolyard kids who kill seem to be like Adam, perpetuating their own sense of inner horror about what might have been done to them.

This journey down the road to revenge has the momentum of a snowball, which gains size and force as it rolls down a snow-covered mountain. The process starts with some form of abuse: verbal, emotional, physical, or sexual. It is paved with the psychological preparation of terror and trauma. And, in the end, all this leads to rage and revenge.

STEP THREE: RAGE AND REVENGE

Even the worst sinner has something he won't do, some line he won't cross. Being made in the image of God gives us the perception that some evil is just too extreme. When the unthinkable—such as the brutal battering of an infant or the sexual molestation of a child—becomes reality, rage takes over human emotions.

When the abuser is too large or too powerful for the abused to strike back, the feelings of wrath are internalized and may lie buried for years. Meanwhile, the victim lives in denial about the seriousness of this inward desire to get even. The rage is stuffed in, bottled up, pushed down into the gut. The conscious mind may not even know these feelings are there. When anyone learns about the abuse and tries to talk about it, the victim may say, "I don't even remember it. I've dealt with it. It's so far in the past it doesn't bother me any more."

Luke Woodham wrote pages that seemed to explain the rage inside him. In a kind of murderous manifesto he described what he would do in the past tense, he was so sure of his determination to do evil. "I killed because people like me are mistreated every day. I did this to show society—'Push us and we will push back.' I suffered all my life. No one every truly loved me."[9]

An internal compromise has been reached. No matter how strange or demonic the activity, the victim feels complete vindication for harboring such ideas. For the moment a first-person-shooter game or involvement in antisocial philosophies (such as satanism with Pearl, Mississippi, killer Luke Woodham, or Nazism and satanism with Columbine killers Harris and Klebold) might offset this suppressed rage.

Now all that's needed for a criminal act to occur is some slighting that gives the victim a substitute target to attack. The original abuser may be dead, absent, or inaccessible. But, in the case of kid killers, someone else takes that person's place. A teacher who reprimanded them. A jock who taunted them. A girlfriend who jilted them. A student clique that ostracized them. Any one of these slights might set off the final act of revenge.

FULL-BLOWN REVENGE

Usually the youth adopts some codified means of justifying the retaliation. For many kids it is *The Satanic Bible,* which teaches that anyone who strikes you on the cheek deserves a fist in the face. Others adopt the cultural viewpoint of misanthropy, which advocates the hatred of all human beings, except your immediate clan or clique. Still others embrace supremacist ideologies by idolizing Adolf Hitler, or anarchistic philosophies by revering mass murderer Charles Manson.

This is the time when the chants of Marilyn Manson, "We love hate, we hate love," fixate in the mind. This is when the blood-splattered video screen of *Doom* turns the teen into a killer. This is also when the young person starts surfing the Web for specific plans on how to build a propane bomb. Diagrams are drawn of which corridors to walk down and which victims to shoot first. Now is the time that the will of the kid killer is resolutely set upon destruction far beyond the imagination of anyone who knows that young person. Calmly and methodically, the plans are being set for an unalterable course of action.

It's at this stage that Andrew Golden and Mitchell Johnson probably stole the guns from Golden's grandfather. This is when Kip Kinkle began building bombs and hid them in his parents' house. This is the point that Eric Harris and Dylan Klebold went to a Denver gun show and asked an older girl to purchase guns for them.

Revenge. They lethally strike back, ignoring God's injunction in Romans 12:19, "Beloved, do not avenge yourselves . . . for it is written, 'Vengeance is Mine, I will repay,' says the Lord."

Kip Kinkle, the Springfield, Oregon, shooter, logged on to the Internet just weeks before the killings and declared his hobbies were, "role-playing games, heavy-metal music, violent TV, throwing rocks at cars." He also said his occupation was, "Surfing the Web for info on how to build bombs." In a literature course he read from a diary in which he had written of his plans to "kill everybody."[10]

Just prior to committing a violent act, the potential kid killer may go through a period of severe self-loathing. He may talk about suicide or enter periods of deep depression. He may turn into a self-mutilator who rips at his flesh with pencil points or hacks his wrists with a razor blade. Before he strikes out violently, he will first try to release the hurt through self-hatred.

But that will not assuage his rage. Only some miracle of intervention will stop his ultimate revenge.

GETTING OFF THE ROAD TO REVENGE

If some young people you know fit anywhere into the pattern I've described in this chapter, intervene immediately. Don't wait for them to ask for help. Be proactive. Don't be afraid you'll offend their sense of privacy. They are desperately waiting for anyone to express a caring concern.

Let them vent their rage. Allow them to talk freely about their intense hatred for their abusers. The first step to true biblical forgiveness is the accurate assessment of blame. In fact, many people never experience real forgiveness because they've never adequately accused those who abused them. Our Lord's Prayer teaches us to forgive our debtors (Matthew 6:12). But no debt can be forgiven until a debt is acknowledged.

From what I know about the kids who killed at school, it seems obvious they never forgave those who wronged them. Luke Woodham never forgave his parents, and the killing of the others that October day in 1997 was possible only after he had plunged a knife into the body of his mother. Kip Kinkle harbored such intense hatred for his parents that the two students he shot at Thurston High School were an afterthought. The real targets of his rage were the mother and father whom he blew away first because he couldn't forgive them for some unknown violation.

Note again the warning signs of this chapter, and wherever you see them, do something before it's too late:

1. Look for evidence of verbal, emotional, physical, or sexual abuse.

2. Listen for a sense of helplessness, which indicates the young person feels victimized.

3. Observe when the rage has turned into actual thoughts of revenge and specific plans have been made to retaliate.

And finally, if you're a parent, don't expect the school to identify a potential problem.

THE CLASSROOM CRISIS

Are you worried that your child might be lost to the conditioning of the culture described in this book? Be prepared. He may already be lost in the environment of big-is-better mega-schools where student bodies number in the thousands. Sure, such institutions offer something for everyone, from carpentry to the culinary arts. What they don't offer in the midst of their state-of-the-art facilities is a sense of connectedness to the real world of virtue and values.

College-size classrooms are the norm in today's major cities and suburbs. These two thousand- to four thousand-person behemoths crowd out the possibility of involvement in extracurricular activities, which can help a student express and define himself. Worse yet, the troubled student with signs of violence, depression, or academic failure will likely be impossible to spot in such an overcrowded, assembly-line high school.

For many students, perhaps your child, school has become a place to congregate and communicate about everything other than education. Cars, clothes, sex, and CDs are more likely to be on your child's mind than history and science. If you're expecting a social worker, counselor, or caring instructor to notice a kid gone bad—perhaps *your* child gone wrong—forget it. It's not likely to happen. The teacher-to-student ratio, let alone the student-to-counselor ratio, may be so out of whack, there is no way any intervention in the life of a troubled child will happen with regularity. Wake up!

If you expect the school to police behavior, let alone understand aberrant conduct, it's not likely to happen. School may just as easily be the place where a child learns to build a bomb as it is where he discovers the joy of intellectual stimulation. Today's educational system makes your job as a parent harder, not easier. Secular schools can't be a fortress from the world. But the Christian home can, and should be.

In Part Three we will look at ways parents can guide their children in a world that's determined to lead them astray.

PART THREE

SOLUTIONS FOR
THE SAVAGERY

CHAPTER 9

INTERVENTION ON TIME

In every case of kids who killed in schools, the parents were dumbfounded by what happened. We may wonder how they could be so clueless about their kids, but they genuinely seemed to be as shocked as anyone. They may have suspected that things weren't exactly as they should be, but they certainly didn't expect their children to commit murder.

The parents of Eric Harris, the Columbine killer, were criticized for being "out of touch." How could anyone's child build a bomb in the garage and leave a sawed-off shotgun on a bedroom dresser shelf and not be noticed? Yet, that's exactly what happened in the Harris home. To get a grip on their child's increasingly difficult life, the Harrises had tried to get Eric enlisted in the Marines. He was rejected when a Marine recruiter visiting their home was told that Eric was taking an antidepressant, Luvox, prescribed for obsessive-compulsive disorder.

And then there was Eric's Web site, a glaring indication of his out-of-control life. On-line he actually threatened to kill classmates and injure as many as possible. In profane, rambling discourses he spouted blasphemies and profanities in the midst of declaring in all-capped type, "DEAD PEOPLE DON'T ARGUE!" The parents of a youth who knew Harris brought these writings to the police. They knew what Harris was saying and were worried. Harris's own parents either weren't sufficiently concerned, or they didn't know what to do. In either case their parenting skills were sorely lacking. But before we pass judgment on the parents of Eric Harris, we should ask ourselves, *How well do we really know our own children?*

I'd like to give parents six warning signs that their child might be in trouble—and then offer suggestions for what they can do before it's too late.

SIX WARNING SIGNS A CHILD MIGHT BE IN TROUBLE

1. OBSESSIVE INVOLVEMENT WITH IMMORAL AND VIOLENT CULTURAL INFLUENCES

Parents have often felt on the cultural defensive. In the 1980s, satanic rock music was blamed for a rise in teen suicides. Through my radio show and counseling with young people, I confirmed that music had played a powerful role in selling the fatalism that blinded the hope of troubled teens. But many parents were reluctant to take my advice and do something about it.

The cultural onslaught continued. Children burned down homes after watching fire-starter episodes of "Beavis and Butt-head." Even younger children explored the occult, prompted by the "Goosebumps" series. To many adults it was one thing after another. About the time they felt informed enough to act on an issue, the world of entertainment had moved on to another evil. The result? Some just gave up on any intervention.

Now families are challenged with a whole new list of threats. Unless a parent is willing to move to Outer Mongolia, the effect of popular culture is hard to escape. And even nomadic tents in the Gobi Desert are now sprouting with generator-powered VCRs. New forms of media are emerging, from digital television to virtual-reality games and an Internet subculture. Immersion-reality diversions are coaching killing behavior.

Now isn't the time to surrender. Intervention is more crucial than ever. The family that avoids the issue may find that a movie or video game will be the last straw to send some kid over the edge in a moment of dark impulsiveness. Therefore, in addition to raising a somewhat sheltered child, the task of parenting is to raise a discerning child. Especially when it comes to the violence glorified all around us.

Kids who kill may be influenced by a single song lyric that codifies their sense of alienation. They may be swayed by a movie or video game that touches their pain at its most vulnerable point. But that film or game didn't cause the pain. The media may teach our children how to more effectively vent their animosities, but it doesn't create the sense of suffering that propels such rage.

Note this difference. When I talk with parents about the Littleton shootings, the conversation is usually about *what* made these kids kill. "Let's get the details, the facts," parents say. Adults seem concerned about how kid killers get even. When I talk to youth about the same shootings, they focus on *why* kids wanted to kill. "Why did these kids become so thirsty for that video game?" kids are asking. "What were they looking for?" Teenagers express deeper thoughts about

139

their inner feelings—wondering what makes a murderer out of a kid who no one thought could kill. Perhaps it's because the young person is thinking about his own frustrations and sees an exaggerated sense of himself in the kid killers. He wouldn't do what a Harris and Klebold did, but he identifies with the negative emotional experiences that cause a kid to latch on to symbols such as Hitler, Marilyn Manson, and brutal video games.

Here is where adults must discern the difference. While the immoral and irresponsible environment of the entertainment media is a legitimate target for frustration, parents must not give in to irrational fears of modern culture. Teenagers have always been drawn to popular culture as a form of alternative social community. I did it with duck tails; you may have worn tie-dyes. Why? We wanted to shock and offend because it was a way of establishing an identity apart from our elders.

But somewhere in the process of such behavior, a line can be crossed. Nonconformity becomes revolt, and the sinful heart of man then has an ideological motive for being different. If carried too far, the trench coat becomes more than a signal of opposition to adult-sanctioned dress. It becomes a tool to embrace evil, extreme evil. And it also crystallizes the desire to get even by putting a form on the feelings of resentment and revenge.

Here is the danger: Parental paranoia, which is heavy-handed and strikes out at symptoms instead of causes, may send a young person toying with dissension off the precipice of real rebellion. Fortunately, most kids make their way back from the edge; they mature and begin to accept their place in pre-adult society; they turn out to be the kids you always knew they could be.

Along the way, the road is bumpy. Teens will test you. At their best they may be sometimes infected with insolence. They will push parents to the limit to see if their values are real or expedient. Every adult hypocrisy will be uncovered and challenged. And if they are themselves challenged, they may retreat to their world of offensive music and cryptic conduct. At that point, the parent must hold steady and pray. I mean, really pray. And the most important prayer is for godly discernment to rightly judge what is truly evil, and to give good guidelines for our children to do the same.

Start by asking questions. "Can you show me the lyrics of that song you're listening to?" "Mind if I play that video game with you?" "Do you think there's a danger you'll get a distorted reality if you watch too much TV?" "What's the most popular movie among your friends?"

Get inside your children's minds and into their world. Be educated. Cultural trends move so quickly, an entertainment danger may have already done its damage before you are sufficiently informed. When you try to reason with a child about altering his entertainment habits, you're dealing with a kid who has already been molded by the media. He is a creature of instant gratification with an incredibly short attention span. Be patient as you try to show your child how his or her values are being affected.

Your enemy is formidable. The typical child in America watches television no less than four to six hours a day. In addition, that same child attends one or more movies, plays countless hours of video games, listens to violent rap and rock music, and watches many more video versions of movies that are typically R-rated. Kids aren't just consuming culture, they are consumed by it. You and your values aren't much competition.

Try to engage your children in mentally and physically challenging activities that break the mold of passivity fostered by today's glut of entertainment opportunities. Get them to think for themselves instead of being force-fed by the humanistic worldview.

2. ABSENCE FROM FAMILY INTERACTION

One of the first signs of trouble is when teens withdraw from family activity. Again, discernment is necessary. All teens tend to look at parents and young siblings with some disdain. And what's good for an elementary school child—like a trip to the zoo—is not appealing to a preteen or teen. So a balance must be found. Some activities for the teen with Mom or Dad might be an alternative to a family outing.

Parents, you also need to talk to your children about what may be bothering them. Get to the bottom of their feelings. You can't do that if you're constantly apart, so address what separates you. Take a vacation, one away from TV or video games. We give our bodies a rest, so why not our senses? Suggest going one day, several days, even a week or more without watching television or playing a video game. Replace that time with relational activities that involve family and friends. You may get to know a stranger in your own home—your child.

Whatever judgments may be made about the Harris and Klebold families, it seems apparent that there was a fundamental disconnection between the troubled world of these children and the lives their parents thought they were leading. The parents thought they were "caring" parents. But sometimes caring isn't enough. There can be no substitute for intimacy fostered by regular "conferences" where family issues are discussed or conversations where honest feelings are expressed or church attendance where spiritual values are emphasized. An open and frank exchange of opinions may be the only time a parent truly shines light into the dark corners of a child's tortured thoughts.

3. ESCAPING INTO A FANTASY WORLD

The mental environment of today's children may put them at risk because they're out of touch with reality. When we played games, they were fantasies of the mind that began and ended in an afternoon. Today's video and role-playing games like *Mortal Kombat* and *Dungeons and Dragons* or *Magic* are an unending fantasy-turned-reality, which some kids live with day and night. So are the chat rooms and other sites kids can access on the Internet.

In the aftermath of Littleton, Paducah, and others, parents are rightfully concerned about what the media is doing to our children. While that apprehension is understandable, we should also ask serious questions about what our children are doing with the media. How are they using it and as a result, what is it doing to them?

The average parent has little realization that the oft-referenced generation gap has a new divide—the media and computer culture. While the media has always been a source of generational alienation, the computer and its ancillary byproducts have widened that gap. Some parents couldn't define Windows from DOS or have no idea how to contact a Web site. In contrast, 11 percent of the world's computer users are under the age of 15. Thirty-six percent of American teens use an online service at home, 49 percent at school, and 69 percent have been on-line at least once in their lifetime, compared to 40 percent of the general population.[1]

Add to this movies like *The Matrix* and *The Basketball*

Diaries, which adults seldom see, blend in the iconography of the Goth subculture, and stir the mixture with a heavy dose of video games like *Doom,* and you have an abyss that is so broad, parents and their children live in different universes. And the universe of the kids who kill kids is a "hyper-mediated" culture of CDs, 150-channel cable TV, and nonstop Web site access; these troubled children can tap into an unlimited number of dark images that further alienate them from adult society.

In fact, in the aftermath of the Columbine shootings, the *Washington Post* reported that 82 percent of Americans blamed the Internet.[2] To be honest, that's an overreaction, a little like blaming the space shuttle for El Niño. The Internet itself isn't evil, but there must be adult supervision if a minor has access to it.

The young are the ruling citizens of the new world order of cyberspace. What divides the generations is this: To adults, the world of computers is a way to balance a checkbook or perform a business function more efficiently. To youth, computers are the entry point for a sphere of life's totality, including recreation, education, and socialization.

That's why I'm not shocked that the parents of kids who have killed knew so little about their offsprings' violent and anti-social sentiments. Much of what these kids really felt inside was expressed in a cultural context where adults seldom intrude—the Internet, chat rooms, Web sites, video games, e-mail. The youth of today have gone where few adults follow. That has to end!

Young people have a desire for empowerment. They want to test their mettle by competing against their peers. They crave social affiliation. All these yearnings can be met in the virtual world apart from the prying eyes of adults. And to a

certain extent, adults do need to respect the "rights" of adolescents to a self-dignity that allows them to test their wings in
their world, in their way. But red flags should be waving when
a child is so self-absorbed in the world of the 'Net that a sense
of community with his or her elders is lost. In that climate, an
at-risk child may go unnoticed until a gun goes off.

Adults must put away their technophobic reactions to
alternative media and lead, or at least follow closely, into the
cyber world of the next millennium. Only then will attentive
adults be able to sort out the signs of childhood mischievous-
ness from indications of an emotional disturbance that could
erupt in dangerous behavior. I suggest that parents of pread-
olescents read the book *Making the Internet Family Friendly*
by Brian Lang and Bill Wilson (Thomas Nelson, 1999).

Children slip in and out of that video game and Internet
ambience until it becomes their everyday life. Get them back
into the real world. Have a family clean-up day at the house.
Go somewhere new and stimulating like a museum or his-
torical site. Involve them in physical activity such as hiking,
biking, or camping. Get them outdoors, where their senses
are in touch with nature.

Another warning sign that a child may be in trouble is
deteriorating physical and psychological health.

4. DETERIORATING PHYSICAL AND PSYCHOLOGICAL HEALTH

Behavioral scientists are just beginning to discover the
amazing degree to which children can internalize feelings
such as anger and depression. And because children may not
be able to express their emotions with words, parents need
to be on the lookout for the signs of emotional disturbances.
Temper tantrums, severe despondency, irritable behavior,
and other dysfunction may be a way of acting out some

internal turmoil. Parents also need to understand the fluidity of a child's feelings, that he or she may act depressed one day and be okay the next. It's the pattern and consistency that's significant. When the mood swings grow deeper and more prolonged, intervention may be necessary.

Too many doctors and psychiatrists may be too quick to suggest mind-altering drugs. Before opting for Prozac, Zoloft, Paxil, Luvox, or Celexa, a parent should ask serious questions about whether such medication will turn his or her child into a permanent patient. If help is in order, increase the degree of intervention before medicating.

So how can you know when it's time to step in and rescue your child? With elementary students look for frequent, unexplained stomachaches, headaches, and fatigue. Watch for significant weight loss or dramatic changes in sleep patterns. Notice if your child's speech is monotone, droning, and lifeless.

In middle school and older children, look for loss of concentration and motivation. Are they dropping out of sports and other activities? Is it taking longer and longer to finish school academic projects? Are personal hygiene and appearance deteriorating? Do they daydream a lot? Do they sleep in frequently and also nap during the day? Of course, in an older child, promiscuity, drug use, even picking at acne and fingernail biting are possible signs that what your child is weathering is more than a passing childhood emotional adjustment.

The key to determining the extent of intervention must rely on more than physical signs, which can be open to highly subjective interpretation. It's the state of the child's soul that a parent must monitor most closely. A child suffering from low self-esteem to the point of frequent teariness or withdrawal could be on the edge. If such actions are accompanied by an obsession with death and dying, intervention (better late than never) is essential.

Don't just focus on what they may be doing, like crying or receding emotionally from the family. Find out what they *feel* like doing, what they'd do if they could, even if such talk turns to thoughts of suicide and violence against others.

There is a telling significance in the words of T. J. Solomon, the Conyers, Georgia shooter. As the assistant principal, Cecil Brinkley, approached Solomon, he put a pistol in his mouth and wept. Then, as he removed the pistol and collapsed, shaking, in the principal's arms, he cried, "I'm so scared."

Our indignity at his actions may cause us to reply, "Give me a break! Because of you we're all scared!"

But potential killers don't normally fall into the embrace of a caring adult after they've just shot six people. They're usually so busy instilling terror, they don't express their own fears. Those three words, "I'm so scared," must have been spoken or expressed to someone, sometime before the lights went out in Georgia. Who wasn't listening who should have been? Who could have intervened before this tragedy-in-progress claimed a curtain call? The most important question is: What child in your care or circle of concern is just as scared, and just as near to becoming the next kid killer?

Experts say that more children are crossing the line that separates sadness from depression, and they're doing it at an earlier age. Children today are under more stress because of factors such as divorce, frequent moves, multiple caretakers, and exposure to violence. In fact, by the time they finish high school, one-fourth of all adolescents have considered suicide.[3] Depressed youth are more prone to abuse drugs and alcohol. Don't wait until the depression reaches the clinical stage. If you see delinquent behavior, constant feelings of sadness, unusual fatigue, morbid thoughts, or sensitivity to failure, get professional help.

5. LEADING A DOUBLE LIFE

Troubled kids—let's face it, even emotionally stable kids—sometimes lead double lives. Remember when you told your mother you were going to a friend's overnight, but the real reason was: "I want to do something my parents won't allow"? Unfortunately, that something can now be drugs or involvement in nefarious activity. Right now politicians are calling for stricter gun-control laws. Mental health professionals say we need more counselors per square kid. Talk show hosts say we need better parents, and the teachers say we need metal detectors at every door. I'm ready to shout, "Will someone please stand up and say, 'We need people looking over the shoulders of our children, spying on their secret lives!'"

Spying? Perhaps that word is a little strong. But we certainly need some scrutiny about their secret activities, which imperil their welfare. The challenge faced by parents today is that the entertainment industry and the climate of our culture has caused our children to be more isolated than ever before from adult input. Consequently, the secrecy of kid culture (secret handshakes and clandestine clubs), which has been a staple of our society, is more dangerous than ever.

A little more than a year before the Columbine incident, another Columbine student, eighteen-year-old Robert Craig, killed his stepfather with a single shot to the head, then fatally shot himself through the roof of his mouth. Craig had a 3.8

grade-point average, a part-time job, and planned to attend college. His mother, Joanne, never suspected her son was so out of control. She now warns, "Kids lead secret lives. Sometimes it's impossible to know them. I thought he was a wonderful kid. He had a close relationship with his stepfather."

Too late, Joanne realizes she should have seen the signs of her son's brooding and his talk of hating school. She knows now that her son told her what she wanted to hear— that everything was fine—not what she needed to know about whatever experience traumatized his life. It's never too late to invade your child's secret emotional life to prevent disaster.

Talk, talk, talk. Over meals. Riding to and from activities. As you're getting ready to leave the house. Capture off-the-cuff moments when their defenses are down. Ask questions. Lots of them. Not intimidating questions, but relational questions about how they perceive their world. Get inside their hurts and disappointments. Don't assume you know how they *really* feel. Hear them out, and be ready to be shocked. You may discover that you have no idea what is really going on in their minds. A survey at Ball State and Columbia universities found that 57 percent of teens who had attempted suicide were found to be suffering from major depression, but only 13 percent of the parents of suicides believed their child was actually depressed.[4]

And a final warning sign that a child might be in trouble is frequent expressions of unresolved anger.

6. FREQUENT EXPRESSIONS OF UNRESOLVED ANGER

While some children in trouble retreat into a private emotional world of reclusive hostility, others are vocal about their bitterness toward life or certain people. Look for triggering behavior, like put-downs or insults by other students, that could cause their conflict to escalate into fights or vicious responses.

Take a zero-tolerance attitude toward violence. If your children express anger about how they're being treated by other students, or by the world in general, quickly get them off the road of such a narcissistic attitude toward life. Let your children know you love them unconditionally, but that such acceptance won't excuse their whining about every injustice that comes their way. Tell them they must earn their right to make it in the real world and that rejection and hardships are part of real life. Replace their anger with the challenge to quit complaining and start winning the respect of their peers. Responsible parents draw clear lines about unacceptable expressions of anger and vindictiveness and enforce moral boundaries, which produce tolerance and forgiveness, even to those who mistreat us.

That said, unresolved anger can be a sign of real problems, the kind we discussed in Chapter 8. I suggest that parents read Dr. Ross Campbell's book *Kids in Danger: Training Your Child to Tame the Destructive Power of Anger* and then get professional counseling.

Perhaps the problem you face isn't with your own child but with someone else's child. There are ten things you should know about your child's friends.

TEN THINGS YOU SHOULD KNOW ABOUT YOUR CHILD'S FRIENDS

In the case of the Jonesboro, Arkansas shootings, it seems clear that Mitchell Johnson strongly persuaded the younger child, Andrew Golden, to plot the shootings. Luke Woodham of Pearl, Mississippi, infamy admits it was Grant Boyette's satanic leadership that compelled him to kill. Eric Harris seemed to sway Dylan Klebold, and those I talked to acknowledged Dylan probably wouldn't have committed the crime without Harris's influence.

What indications should you look for that an acquaintance of your child is having a bad influence? Here are ten things to watch for in your child's friends.

1. APPEARANCES. Do your child's friends dress in black? Does their appearance affect a dark, somber demeanor? What about T-shirts with negative slogans? For example, it has been reported that when Marilyn Manson first started out, promoters sold T-shirts at his concerts with the message: "Kill God, Kill Your Parents, Kill Yourself." Eric Harris and Dylan Klebold wore T-shirts with Nazi slogans. Multiple body piercings, demonic tattoos, and satanic jewelry (pentagrams, goats heads, skulls) are signs of rebellion and possible direct involvement in the occult.

2. SECRECY. Does your child spend time with questionable peers without telling you what he's doing? Beware if your child is vague about who he was with and what they did. Be suspicious that criminal acts, drug usage, or occult activity might be involved. The parents of every kid killer said their child must have had a secret life of some kind. Dylan Klebold's father was a strong gun-control advocate and couldn't imagine how his son amassed the weaponry to do what he did.

3. DANGEROUS LITERATURE. Do you ever spot your child's friends carrying books, or loaning books to your child that you wouldn't want them to read? Some examples are: *The Satanic Bible*, *The Necronomicon*, *Mein Kampf*, *The Terrorist's Handbook*, *The Anarchist's Cookbook*, or any book on witchcraft or satanism. Kids often get their anti-social attitudes from outlaw books that advocate violence and revenge. You may not allow these books in your home, but a friend may introduce them to your child. Don't be like the parents in those two witchcraft cases mentioned in Chapter 7 who were more concerned about their children's legal rights than about their dabbling in witchcraft. If your child's friends are into Wicca or satanism, your child is probably there too. Get spiritual help.

4. RECREATIONAL ACTIVITIES. Watch out for friends who introduce your children to games that are violent or occult in nature. You may not permit games like *Doom* to be played on a computer in your home, but what if your child has access to such on a friend's computer? You may not have permitted your child to play *Dungeons and Dragons,* but he may meet with peers who do play the game outside your home. Don't just know who your child's friends are—know what they do to pass time.

5. CONCERTS. Too many parents drop their kids off at concerts because they are "going to meet some friends there." Find out what kind of concert they're attending and insist on meeting their friends. One glance at the way their friends look will tell you a lot about the kind of concert they're going to. Tell your child he needs friends who will go with him to Christian music concerts where positive spiritual values are extolled. Several Christian artists like Amy Grant and Michael W. Smith have crossed over into the pop market. Introduce your child to these artists and other Christian singers, like Crystal Lewis and D.C. Talk, as early as possible. Music reaches all of us—and influences us—more than we will ever know.

6. MOVIES AND RENTAL VIDEOS. Did the parents of Michael Carneal have any idea their son had watched the R-rated video *The Basketball Diaries*? Perhaps it wasn't shown in their home, but Michael might have seen it at a friend's house, especially one of the members of the occult group he associated with. If a friend of your child invites him to see a movie like *The Matrix* (which features a scene with chilling similarities to the Columbine killings), tell your child that he doesn't need friends like that. Encourage your child to avoid friends who are attracted to violent films.

7. COMMUNICATION WITH ACQUAINTANCES. A wise parent won't consider it an invasion of privacy to check out a child's room to look for handwritten exchanges with a dangerous acquaintance. Know who your child is carrying on any kind of communication with, whether it is written or electronic. If you find notes in secret languages, codes, or symbols, your child may be hanging out with someone involved in satanic activity. Also check your child's e-mail. Children can be contacted by unsavory characters who hide behind the anonymity of the Internet.

8. BEWARE OF FRIENDS FROM TROUBLED HOMES. It's always safer to have your child befriend peers from a Christian home with a two-parent family. Many single parents do a fine job of child rearing, but some struggle to overcome the emotional damage to their children. Mitchell Johnson, the older kid killer in Jonesboro, Arkansas, was bitter about his parents' divorce and complained that he seldom saw his biological father. Luke Woodham, who shot the students in Pearl, Mississippi, suffered from tragic family dynamics, in which he claims his mother blamed him for her divorce. A child with that kind of baggage could negatively infect your child with a jaded view of life.

9. BEWARE OF OLDER FRIENDS. Messed-up older kids sometimes prey on younger students to get control over them. Watch out for kids in their early twenties who don't go to college, work at part-time jobs, live alone, and hang out with a rough crowd. They act out their own powerlessness by dominating a younger, easily impressed child. Grant Boyette did that to Luke Woodham.

10. ENCOURAGE SPIRITUAL FRIENDSHIPS. Teach your child to forge friendships with those who have positive values. He'll be more likely to find those peers in church-related activities. A friendship founded on a common faith will have a spiritual focus, whereas a bond that results from deviant behavior will be destructive. As my friend Michael W. Smith says in his song "Friends," which he sang at the Columbine High School memorial service, "Friends are friends forever if the Lord's the Lord of them."

Although I don't feel that parents are entirely to blame for their children's actions, more and more people are calling for parental accountability. Whether it is right or wrong, parents are beginning to be held legally responsible for their children's actions.

PARENTAL LIABILITY

The blood on the steps of Columbine High had barely dried when the parents of Isaiah Shoels made a call to Geofrey Fieger, the attorney of Jack Kevorkian, Mr. Assisted Suicide. Fieger, who had vehemently attacked Christians and had vigorously defended Kevorkian's right to deal death, was ready to take their lawsuit. Even though he had previously shown full support for Kevorkian's right to terminate life, Fieger displayed no conflict with opposing the rights of Dylan Klebold and Eric Harris to finish off their victims. Apparently Fieger's moral compass differentiated between a syringe with a lethal injection and a sawed-off shotgun. Fieger asked for $250 million from the parents of Klebold and Harris for not preventing the death of Isaiah.

The parents of Isaiah Shoels aren't the first to get in on the action. Parents of the school gunmen in Jonesboro, Arkansas, Paducah, Kentucky, and Moses Lake, Washington, all face substantial lawsuits from families of the victims. The suits allege they should have done more to supervise their children.

Though the parents of some shooters, such as Kip Kinkle, had apparently taken extraordinary measures to reach a troubled child, society's prevailing view of who is to blame has shifted in the aftermath of the Columbine killings. The topic of parental responsibility is frequent fodder for talk shows and editorials. In the minds of many, the parents of a kid who kills aren't also victims, they are accomplices. The prevailing opinion has shifted from *There but for the grace of God go I* to *If you're not going to control your kids, we're going to control you!*

Local governments are getting the message. An Oklahoma law requires parents to complete community service or pay a fine of $2,000 if their child possesses a firearm at school. Florida requires parents to pay the cost of their child's criminal prosecution, and in Tennessee, parents must pay the cost of medical exams, treatment, and pretrial placement of their children. Twenty-three states have extended some form of legal sanctions against parents whose children commit crimes. Thirteen states, including Colorado, make parents criminally liable for failing to supervise delinquent children. On the federal level, the White House has recommended making it a felony for parents to knowingly or recklessly allow children to use guns to commit a crime. So far, no parent has actually been convicted of a crime committed by his or her children, and charges are seldom filed by prosecutors. But lawyers obviously have no compunction about filing lawsuits based on accidental or "intentional" assistance.

Constitutionally, the real issue is proving that a parent should have known there was a substantial risk his child might commit a crime and did nothing to prevent it. Still, proponents of parent responsibility argue that the best place to begin crime prevention is in the home.

But how culpable can a parent be when an adolescent's own mind and his own decisions compel actions a mother and father would never condone? What about all the child has learned from society and culture about violence? How many children have hidden their true thoughts from their parents? And before we go after Mom and Dad, shouldn't we first censure Hollywood, the television networks, and the makers of violent video games?

Yet there is reason to infer that parental responsibility laws have a scriptural basis. From Exodus to Ephesians the consistent message of God's Word is that parents must continually remind their children of God's laws and train their offspring in the ways of the Lord. One might conclude that it would be scripturally appropriate to levy some punitive sanctions against the parents of a criminally motivated child, but any ultimate accountability is on the head of the child. Under levitical law, the child who blasphemed was himself stoned, not the parents. In the New Testament context, the child is to honor his father and mother if he wishes a long life.

The biblical distinctive between what one person allows and what another person actually does, is ingrained in our legal common law system of justice. It would be dangerous to breach this wall of differentiation out of a passion to make someone pay for the killing of our kids. Existing laws already address the liability of those who actually aid, abet, or contribute to the delinquency of a minor. Any other criminal penalties seem an overreaction.

However, civil penalties are plausible. The threat of making bad parents pay for court costs and restitution should be more stringently enforced. And, as much as I dislike the increasing litigiousness of our society, parents may deserve to be sued. But such civil suits are a far cry from allowing courts, which are already too interventionist in family life, to have yet another foot in the door of the government's creeping control over the sanctity of the home.

What's needed more than punishment is encouragement for greater involvement of parents in the lives of their children. As a nation we must reassert our understanding that parents are the primary influence on their children's values. It isn't just a responsibility, it is a duty of parents to know, even if some judicious snooping is required, when a child is at risk. Parents, not the government, must inoculate their offspring from the destructive effects of popular culture. Leaving children unsupervised for extended periods of time and allowing them to spend hours on the Internet without knowing what sites they visit is an abdication of a parent's responsibility. Above all, we have to get back to the idea that parents are obligated to correct the behavior of their children and guide them in a world that's determined to lead them astray.

CHAPTER 10

ANSWERS TO EXTREME EVIL

In what has become a ritual in the aftermath of school killings, we are accustomed to the photographs of emotionally strained students returning to pick up their belongings. They trudge quietly into school, accompanied by parents or counselors. They enter sober and exit weeping. They look away from the bullet-scarred walls and the windows where broken glass has been replaced by plywood. They pick up pencils, backpacks, art objects, and gym clothes. For some it's a relief; for others, a reminder of fear and loss.

At Columbine High School, the students were led into the gymnasium where their belongings were unceremoniously arranged in white, numbered garbage bags. They walked over carpet that had chunks ripped up, evidence gathered by the crime scene crew. They congregated noiselessly to quickly identify their belongings. Some couldn't help but wonder if their sense of safety in life had been shattered forever. Whatever they saw would never be the same. In certain rooms that had the most carnage, officials had promised a complete renovation so that the same space couldn't be recognized again when the students returned.

As the students emerged from school, the consensus of most was that this was the beginning of getting on with the rest of life. But how sad that they ever had to enter such a scene. If those who could have, and should have, cared about our kids had been there in time to intervene, this scene of sadness would never have happened. It doesn't have to happen again.

Even though we live in a cursed generation, afflicted by materialism and plagued by rampant neglect and abuse, today's youth yearn to be blessed. In the beginning when God made man, He pronounced favor on humanity. "So God created man in His own image; in the image of God He created him; male and female He created them," Genesis 1:27 proclaims. The next verse says, "Then God blessed them."

The heritage of humanity is "blessing," which comes from the Hebrew word *barach* meaning to "salute" or "congratulate." Think of it! God Almighty, Creator of the Heavens and the entire Universe, looked upon man whom He had framed from Earth's dust and declared, "You are blessed! I salute you!"

THE HERITAGE OF BLESSING

Do the children among us know they are blessed? Of course not. Most don't even know they are creatures of value. As a culture, we don't bless our children—we curse them with too much of everything, and not enough of the right things. We curse them with violent entertainment and pornographic stimulation. We curse them with an education that ignores God and replaces the divine with the profane. We tell them they are descended from animals and then chafe when they act like brute beasts. No wonder they act out in violent ways. Their fury is the only way they know to get attention. We have cursed them, so they curse us. And they kill each other . . . But a better day is coming!

The prophet Malachi foretold our time. In chapter four, verses 4–6, he announced at the end of the ages that God would "turn the hearts of the fathers to the children, And the hearts of the children to their fathers."

It's time to lift the curse. Parents need to turn to their children and confess they have sinned against them by failing to give attention and approval when it was needed most. They have sinned by adding to the curse through spiritual indifference instead of diminishing the curse by godly guidance. The Jewish people have a beautiful way of communicating the importance of proper parental relationships.

In devout Jewish homes, at Sabbath meal, the mother and father lay hands on each child and give them a spoken blessing. This invocation serves two purposes. First it is a proclamation of the child's value. Second, it pronounces the favor of the parents who express a sense of esteem toward their offspring. This superb expression of love and respect can be copied by a simple touch or a warm hug. When you reach out to embrace your children and say, "I love you," you are blessing them and breaking the curse of our culture.

But the blessing needs to go further.

We must bless by instructing our children in the paths of virtue. Mothers must never be too busy, or too involved in their own careers, to nurture their children. Likewise, fathers must take time to provide even-handed authority in the face of unruly behavior. In addition to the consistency necessary to enforce these nourishing examples, it's important to impress our children with valued behavior by emphasizing it.

Some families choose to memorialize their children's passages through life with significant ceremonies. As with Jewish families who hold to the tradition of the Bar Mitzvah, the rites of maturing grant our children both opportunities and responsibilities. It is a means by which we may say to them, "I acknowledge your transition by bestowing more liberties and demanding more obligations." The ceremony can be as simple as the passing on of a family heirloom at a significant age or as touching as a dad's night out with his daughter or a mother's special day set aside for her son.

In some Jewish homes an important dinner or reception is held and the children may be lifted up on a chair to express their elevation of worth in the family. Then the father says, "This is my beloved son (or daughter). I am pleased with him (or her)." (If you are interested in passing on a blessing to your children, you might want to read the book *The Gift of the Blessing* by Gary Smalley and John Trent.)

In whatever way we choose, we must find a way to "elevate" our children. The child who is dropped off at a Marilyn Manson concert isn't being elevated. The kid who builds bombs in the basement because Mom and Dad are never around to know what he's up to is being debased. The student who spends more time playing violent video games than he spends talking to his parents is being devalued. The curse falls only on those who don't know they are blessed.

THE PURPOSE OF PARENTING

Do we really love our children? This question isn't rhetorical; I really want an answer. The school killings beg for an answer.

Why are kids killing kids? Why are schools constantly facing bomb threats, hit lists of potential victims, and fears that classes will have to be cancelled because of rumors that some disgruntled child bears a murderous grudge? Would children who know they are really loved do something like that?

Many people, especially Christians, have been reluctant to criticize the parents of kid killers. There is genuine compassion for parents who suffer both the loss of their child through death or imprisonment, as well as having to live with the realization that their child has robbed other parents of their precious offspring. Such charity is admirable, but we must not let it get in the way of raising serious issues that will give guidelines for the rest of us who don't want that happening in our homes.

We have allowed the parents of kid killers to grieve in silence and privacy. But perhaps the time has come for an accounting. They owe us any explanation they have that will help good to emerge from such evil. They have to move beyond shame and sorrow to tell us what they do know about why their kids killed. Give it to us straight. For those who have died, and for those who might die, we are owed that much.

As a society it may be time to even get tough on the parents of kid killers. We shame those who beat, neglect, starve, and physically abandon their offspring. We even arrest and prosecute them. The least that we can do is to publicly disgrace those parents who pose a threat to our communities by their indolent attitude toward their children's welfare.

Finally, parents can be a blessing to each other and to their neighborhoods by taking a more proactive stand in their communities. I'd like to suggest seven ways parents can protect their neighborhoods, their schools, and their families.

SEVEN WAYS TO PROTECT YOUR NEIGHBORHOOD, SCHOOL, AND FAMILY

What can you do to make your cities and neighborhoods safer, to avoid the threat of your communities harboring the next kid killer?

1. REPORT CRIMINAL BEHAVIOR TO AUTHORITIES. Speak up. Be bold. If you see a child doing something violent or criminal, report it immediately. In Littleton, Randy and Judy Brown downloaded fifteen pages from Eric Harris's menacing Web site and took it to authorities after Harris threatened to kill their son, Brooks. For more than a year on the Internet, Harris had threatened to "kill and injure as many as I can." He described the explosives he and Klebold had built. The Browns each had called the sheriff's office six to eight times and even talked to a member of the bomb squad. Unfortunately, the matter was never properly handled; however, you can be assured that, in the aftermath of the Columbine killing, police departments will probably have a different response.

2. EDUCATE OTHERS ABOUT THE DANGERS OF THE MEDIA. Fourteen years ago, Tipper Gore wrote, "Rock music has become pornographic and sexually explicit, but many parents are unaware of the words their children are listening to, dancing to, doing homework to, falling asleep to."[1] Gore's warning remains even more relevant today, even though her political agenda has since compromised her outspokenness. If you know about a dangerous rock group, movie, or video game, don't hesitate to inform your friends. Many of them may never have heard of artists like Marilyn Manson. They may be unaware of the gratuitous violence in movies like *The Matrix*. Get information yourself about dangerous aspects of the media, and then instruct others.

3. LEARN ABOUT INTERNET FILTRATION SYSTEMS. Since many children get their ideas about hate groups, pornography, and building bombs from the Internet, check out what Net-nanny systems are available and pass the word around. Several Christian companies offer excellent filtration devices that will keep objectionable material away from children. (One of the best is with Lifeline, the Christian long-distance telephone company: call 1-800-805-0506 for details.) Encourage other parents to not allow their children unsupervised access to home computers. In fact, having the family computer(s) in a open area where anyone using them can be observed by all family members is one way to avoid the secrecy that leads to the abuse of the Internet. The book *Making the Internet Family Friendly* (Thomas Nelson, 1999) discusses the different filtration options so it can also be a resource for you.

4. HELP OTHER FAMILIES TO RID THEIR HOMES OF EVIL INFLUENCE. Talk to your friends about taking drastic action in their homes. Accompany them on a search-and-destroy operation in the rooms of their children. Tear down posters that glorify evil. Discard CDs, movies, and video games that encourage violence. Cassie Bernall, who died a martyr's death in the Columbine killings, was a rebellious teenager involved in witchcraft a few years earlier. Her parents actively intervened and took authoritarian action, demanding that she go to church and that she cut off all contact with her bad friends. Without their active involvement, her life would have deteriorated further. Imagine how they'd feel today if she had been killed in that spiritual condition. If someone you know is reluctant to intervene in the life of a troubled child, urge them to be proactive.

5. REPORT PROBLEM CHILDREN TO EACH OTHER. Make a pact with other parents whose children attend the same school. Agree to report to each other whenever any one of you sees a child posing a potential threat. Your child may tell you what another dangerous child says or does that parents of that child may not know. Go to that child's parent with the information. If you've agreed in advance to do this, you'll avoid hesitation because you think the parent might be offended. Wouldn't you want to know if your child was exhibiting menacing behavior? Other parents undoubtedly feel the same. Support each other with this compact by agreeing to help the parent-in-crisis with whatever support is needed.

The Harris and Klebold killers built dozens of bombs over the course of a year. They spent hours playing violent video games, even creating a version of the game using the floor plan of Columbine High. The killers posted their intentions on the 'Net, they wore T-shirts glorifying hate, they spoke openly of their devotion to Hitler. How this could have happened without the parents being aware we may never know. Perhaps their preoccupation with other issues kept them from giving these boys attention and guidance. In fact, the parents may have suspected their children were on the edge. Before any victims or suspects had been identified in the shootings, Dylan Klebold's father, Tom, called police to offer assistance, saying he suspected his son was involved. The parents of Harris and Klebold obviously lived in denial. If you know of parents who are not facing reality, say something. The risk of offending such parents is less important that the possibility of facing a far more gruesome truth later.

6. DECLARE YOUR SUPPORT FOR SCHOOL OFFICIALS TO TAKE DECISIVE ACTION. After Littleton, a series of copycat incidents resulted in bomb threats and kids talking about their hatred of athletes and teachers, with the implied threat of harm. In one instance, high school students used a Web site to congratulate the killers. In many cases the students involved were suspended or interrogated by authorities.

What happened then? In some cases school officials faced angry parents and the American Civil Liberties Union, which threatened legal action. Fight against the idea that kids have a right to express themselves no matter how offensive their actions may be. Let your school teachers and administrators know that you'll back their efforts to prevent bullying, taunting, sexual harassment, and talk of violent reprisals during school hours. If they know they have the support of parents in the community, school personnel act more affirmatively.

7. ENCOURAGE MOTHERS TO STAY AT HOME AS MUCH AS POSSIBLE. In the past three decades the time mothers spend working outside the home has doubled. The national average of hours mothers are absent from the home working for pay is 1200 hours per year.[2] Even a small portion of those 1200 hours invested in the activities of their children would make a significant moral and spiritual difference. That time represents hours mothers are not in touch emotionally with their children and are unable to monitor their behavior. In the case of Dylan Klebold, his mother, Sue, worked with physically disabled kids. While such a commitment is admirable, she surely feels regret that she failed to be more directly involved in the life of her own emotionally disabled son. Without judging her actions, it is fair to ask what lives might have been saved if she had watched her son saying "Heil, Hitler!" during bowling class and noticed him wearing swastikas to school.

Now that I've said all this, I must say that I'm not advocating "Big Brother Is Watching You," a society where everyone is everyone else's watchdog. However, parents throughout the years have been more involved in the lives of their children and their neighbors' children. General Colin Powell certainly experienced that as he was growing up in South Bronx. His thoughts about parenting were very pertinent to our current problems.

WHERE ARE THE AUNTS?

"I don't watch much television, but when I do, I watch those *National Geographic* specials. The ones with the animals," Colin Powell said at our dinner meeting. He was reflecting further on Littleton and drew upon an illustration based on life in the animal kingdom he had seen in these specials.

"Watch the way a mother lion cares for her cubs," General Powell said. "She lets them play actively with seemingly little concern. They bite, they growl, they rough and tumble, but there are boundaries. When a cub gets out of line, they get swatted with her powerful paw. They're given liberties, but there's a limit."

Colin Powell smiled. He really did like those animal television specials. But then he turned sober. "We're not doing to our children what animals do to their offspring."

He grew reflective. "I remember how it was done when I was a kid growing up in the South Bronx. Everyone was an aunt."

He obviously noted the confused look on my face, so he took the explanation further.

"No matter where I was in the neighborhood, there was an aunt looking out of some window. Oh, I don't mean they were all actually my aunts. They just took on that responsibility. Every mother looked after every other mother's son as if he were her own. Every mother was an aunt, part of our culture's extended family. Even if my mother wasn't watching, some other woman was. She was like that lioness, 'swatting' us into line."

"Where are the aunts in our society today?" I asked.

General Powell nodded. "That's a good question, Bob. That's a good question."

Those aunts were there because they believed in life, not death. Life that springs from values that understand right and wrong are the building blocks of society. They knew that an obsession with death results from the lack of a caring community. Unfortunately, our current culture of death has created a social pathology where children have no safe place from their fears. No aunts are looking over their shoulders and reminding them of the boundaries that keep away death and fear.

Chapter 11

IT'S A GOD THING

When a tragedy like the Columbine High School shoot-ings strikes, some wonder, *Where is God in all of this? Is He sleeping? Does He really care? Why does He allow such violence and injustice?*

Believe me, God has not been asleep in Littleton. Three months after the shootings the *Rocky Mountain News* pub-lished a feature article entitled "It's a God Thing." This article told the story of Revival Generation, a Littleton-based teenage prayer movement that began two years ago to help students take advantage of a 1990 U.S. Supreme Court ruling that said public schools must provide religious clubs the same access as private groups.

By the time the Littleton shootings occurred, this move-ment had seeded more than 350 prayer clubs in Colorado and several other states, one of which was at Columbine High School. And after the shootings students from this movement began receiving numerous invitations to witness about their faith at teen events in Littleton and across the counrty.

"Satan was probably pretty upset that, when he opened that box, we sent a message back to him that we're gonna

171

turn this thing around," Josh Weidmann, founder of the movement, said.[1]

There can be no mistaking these kids' dedication. They are as serious as the shooters who gunned down their classmates. As our culture coarsens, more and more teenagers are returning to the church and faith. At one mainline summer church camp in Colorado that normally draws several hundred kids, 1600 showed up after Columbine. To say that triumph has arisen from tragedy would be an understatement. Revival, real revival, old-fashioned heaven-sent revival is evident everywhere, because Eric Harris and Dylan Klebold killed.

It's a God thing.

Oprah booked Columbine kids who love Jesus. *Newsweek* featured a story. *Time* noted the movement. The article "It's a God Thing" in the *Rocky Mountain News* stated, "When the two killers opened their Pandora's box of horrors, they seem to have unintentionally sparked a Christian revolution."[2]

The inspiration for these radical kids for Christ has been the stories of faith that came out of Columbine. Earlier in the book you heard about the martyrdom of Cassie Bernall and Rachel Scott, but they weren't the only ones.

JOHN TOMLIN'S TESTIMONY

John Tomlin, sixteen, was the kid in the Green Bay Packers shirt whom Harris and Klebold killed. John, who had recently been on a missionary trip to Mexico, was home-schooled until a year ago. He was a quiet kid who, the night before he was killed, spent an hour on the phone with his girlfriend—praying!

A young woman, who remembers his last moments alive, had herself been shot nine times. She was next to him in the cafeteria when the shooters sought their next victim. Both were under a table when Harris and Klebold entered the room. When the shoes of the shooters stepped in front of the table, John stood. Then he was dead. His parents faced the national media in the days after Littleton and declared, "We have hope because of Jesus Christ." Hardened news anchors wept.

It's a God thing.

THE STORY OF RACHEL SCOTT'S BROTHER

In the days after the killing of Rachel Scott, her father and brother spoke openly about the significance of her martyrdom. To packed churches and in front of television cameras from around the world, her father, Darrell, declared, "I've always heard the cliché that a parent should not outlive their child, but now I'm a living example of that. There is a peace that God has for those who know Him that passes understanding. The grace of God is sufficient for the moment. It's not something you can store up; it's just there when it's needed. God is using the Columbine situation for a tremendous move of God throughout this country and around the world."[3]

When a cynical news reporter asked Darrell where his God was that day, he responded, "At the same place He was when His own Son was killed, and at the same place He was when my son was spared."

Darrell's son, Craig, was also in the shooters' line of fire that day. His life was spared. In fact, Craig was in the library, where the main carnage occurred. When he first heard the shots, he thought it was a senior prank. Then a youth walked in the door, bleeding from a gunshot wound, and fell to the floor. Craig dived under a desk. Sixteen-year-old Matt Kechter was on one side, and eighteen-year-old Isaiah Shoels was on the other. As he listened, Craig heard both Cassie Bernall and Valerie Schnurr confess their faith in God, and

173

then they were shot. Harris and Klebold walked toward Craig and shot to death both Shoels and Kechter. Craig pretended he was dead.

In his own words, Craig described what happened next: "My ears were ringing from the shots. I couldn't hear anything. I asked God for courage to take away my fear. As soon as I prayed that, it happened. Then God spoke to me—I literally heard His voice. He told me, 'Get out of there.'

"I helped some kids get out of there. Then I turned around and saw a girl who had been shot in the shoulder. Her shoulder was almost completely gone. She rocked back and forth on the ground in shock, saying, 'Help me!' I put my arm around her neck and my arm around her waist, and I helped her out of the library. We all ran out an emergency exit toward a cop car in a field about thirty yards away.

"As soon as we got behind the cop car, Harris and Klebold came back to the library, where I had been. They exchanged gunfire with the cops, and then killed themselves. The investigators told me that they killed themselves because they ran out of victims to kill. I saw so many of my peers praying. Kids you would never see do that. They were always thinking about their image. But they just realized what mattered, and they prayed."[4]

It's a God thing.

THE WITNESS OF RACHEL SCOTT

What Craig says about his sister's love for people may be the most important lesson of Columbine. He points out how accepting she was of everyone. "She would have been the perfect friend for Eric and Dylan," Craig says. "They needed someone to accept them, to have some positive ground with them. Rachel would have done that, but they killed her."

A friend of Darrell Scott, Rachel's father, a professional musician who once played with Bob Seger's Silver Bullet Band, wrote a song in Rachel's memory. Her life inspired the lyricist to remember how so many had been touched by her love for God and others. The refrain expressed the meaning of Rachel's death by declaring how her martyrdom had brought others to their knees, to confess faith in Christ. When I first heard the song, I was struck by the way that one teenage girl had moved the lives of so many.

My mind goes back to the girl whose story introduced this book, the one who wept beside Rachel's car. She was, in fact, brought to her knees by the power of Rachel's witness. The shooters were not.

Dylan Klebold experienced Rachel's witness. He saw the pantomime Rachel Scott performed in school the year before. Rachel danced to the Ray Boltz song, "Watch the Lamb," a powerful portrayal of Christ's sacrificial atonement. Klebold ran the sound for Rachel's performance. He heard the words. Her father, Darrell, wept that day, almost prophetically, but Dylan didn't. Klebold sat unmoved, imbibing his favorite alcoholic drink—Aftershock, a potent cinnamon-flavored spirit. He always got buzzed when he did sound. He didn't know then that *Rachel* means "little lamb" and that he would execute the sacrifice—Rachel, the lamb, pointing to Christ, the Lamb of God.

Three days before the shooting, Eric Harris was among seventy skinheads and Goth street kids attending a Christian concert. Before the band played that night, a pastor stood to speak. "Somebody in here has either murdered someone or is about to," he said. "Please reconsider and accept the Lord. God can save you out of that lifestyle, clean you up, and take you out of that." Eric Harris could have given his life to Christ that night. He clearly had the opportunity to silence the raging in his mind. He didn't, but God gave him the chance.

It's a God thing.

IT'S OUR THING

Four days before Rachel died, her family had a conversation like none they'd ever had. For two hours the family poured out their love toward one another. Darrell remembers putting his head down on the table, with Rachel sitting across from him, and sobbing. They cried, they hugged. God gave them a goodbye they didn't know they were getting at the time. Rachel wrote in her diary, "God, use me. God, fill my life with passion. God, fill my life with purpose. God, let me reach the unreached."

He did. When Rachel's funeral was beamed to a watching world, her friends again performed the same mime. Millions stopped what they were doing to "watch the lamb."

It's a God thing.

Now it's our thing. We must make the world see God's love for every creature, especially the Eric Harrises and Dylan Klebolds among us. Politicians won't do it. Teachers can't do it. Hollywood refuses to do it. You and I must point them to the Lamb.

We must pray. At home, on the job, and even in school. They can't stop us. No law can silence the cry of the heart. They prayed in Columbine that dreadful day. We must pray every day.

And we must act. Littleton caused the nation to stop on a dime. No one cared what the Dow was doing that day. The American dream became a nightmare. We remembered what matters in a most catastrophic way. Suddenly no one was afraid to talk about faith. The spiritual axis of life was immediately arighted. An entire nation realized that belief in God and personal responsibility were important after all. The usual shrug of the shoulders about "kids at risk" was turned into action to console the wounded and dying. We acted then and we have to keep on acting.

We must also proclaim. Harris and Klebold didn't have to do what they did. They didn't come from broken homes. They had other siblings who didn't turn out that way. Their families were upscale with every advantage. But they made a choice—a choice to rebel and defy. A choice to mock, a choice to kill.

On April 20, 1998, exactly one year prior to the day she was killed, Rachel Scott, like Cassie Bernall, wrote an almost prophetic expression of her faith. Rachel's parents made copies of her diary entry public to demonstrate how God had prepared her for what would come. Rachel mentioned, without regret, how her uncompromising stand for the Lord had alienated some of her classmates. She declared that nothing would stop her from telling others about Jesus, even if she had to sacrifice everything she had. Rachel's words reflected a spiritual depth normally expressed by someone far beyond her adolescent years. With a firmness and fervor she was willing to lose every friend she had if she could please her best friend, Jesus.

The voices of Rachel Scott, Cassie Bernall, and John Tomlin cry out. Are you listening?

It's a God thing. Now it's your thing.

A PARENTAL POSTSCRIPT

I was restless. Our eighteen-month-old had been up all night. Her fever was almost 102°. Mom held her in our bed to keep her from crying. It wasn't life-threatening. Just an earache. But very painful for an infant. The kind of trial every parent knows about and remembers.

I couldn't sleep, so I went to my computer to write this chapter. As I sat typing at 3:00 A.M., the door to my home office opened and our four-year-old stumbled in. I don't know if she heard her sister's cries or somehow sensed the tension in the household. She was scared and couldn't sleep.

"Daddy, would you come cuddle me and pray with me?"

I knew what she wanted. Every night when we say prayers we end by asking, "Put big strong angels around my bed to protect me and keep the devil away." This night she had fallen asleep early, before I had a chance to tuck her in bed and pray. That missing link was what she needed to ease her troubled mind.

I left off the writing of the words above, took her in my arms, and carried her upstairs to her bedroom. She snuggled up to me and hung on tightly. I prayed. She nodded off. But each time she did, and I tried to gently ease myself out of her bed, she'd grab me again.

In those early morning hours, I struggled to be so certain what you'd read would affect you as it affected me. I cried. I wiped tears from my eyes with every line. I remembered that Cassie Bernall's grandmother had once worked for me in our ministry. She was a good woman. A godly woman who passed on a heritage that found root in Cassie's life. That link, indirect though it was, tied me to this tragedy.

So did my daughter's unyielding grip. I hung on to her too. In the world we live in, I realized I might have to some-day let her go. I prayed that it would not be in the same way as Brad and Misty Bernall and Darrell and Craig Scott.

I just knew that I had to be willing, just as Rachel and

Cassie and John were willing. Just as God was willing to let go of His Son for our sakes.

When I finally crept out of my daughter's room, I paused by her bedroom door to glance back one more time at her. She slept so peacefully. Now she knew the angels were there, and so was her daddy. No matter what extreme evil raged all around her, she was surrounded by extreme Love, unconditional Love, the Love that never lets go and never leaves.

It truly is a God thing.

APPENDIX

Here is a listing of some of the other copycat situations where kids were stopped before any killing occurred.

Where: Wilkes-Barre, Pennsylvania
When: May, 1999
Who: Internet chat group
What: Bomb threat
Result: School classes cancelled

Where: Spotswood, New Jersey
When: May, 1999
Who: Unidentified eighteen-year-old
What: Threatened to blow up high school
Result: Student arrested

Where: Burlington, Wisconsin
When: May, 1999
Who: Five boys including a fifteen-year-old boy known as a devil-worshipper who had 666 tattooed on his right forearm

What: Detailed plot to kill school officials and a dozen students

Result: Three boys arrested and charged with conspiracy to commit first-degree intentional homicide

Where: Allen, Texas
When: May 13, 1999
Who: Unidentified students
What: Eleven anonymous bomb threats to school; high school, two middle schools, and elementary school evacuated
Result: School board at first shut classes down for remainder of school year as a ruse to fool the culprits, but then reversed the decision

Where: Denver, Colorado
When: May 14, 1999
Who: Fifteen-year-old freshman at Kennedy High School
What: Threatened to kill classmates and a teacher and blow up the school. Had detailed plans to handcuff people on a hit list to their desks and "blow their hands off or shoot them in the head." Said it would be "Columbine all over again."
Result: Student arrested and charged with felony menacing

Where: Adams County, Colorado
When: May 14, 1999
Who: Four unidentified teenagers
What: Planned to copycat Columbine. Informant pro-

vided written plans, detailed drawings, and a map of the school building being targeted.

Result: Four teens charged as adults with multiple felony counts, including attempted first-degree murder and conspiracy to commit first-degree murder.

Where: Brazil, Indiana
When: May 14, 1999
Who: Thirteen-year-old boy
What: Exploded a pipe bomb because of a grudge with a girl at school. Six other bombs were planted on vehicles owned by the girl's father.
Result: Student arrested

Where: West Palm Beach, Florida
When: May 15, 1999
Who: Unknown
What: Prom night for Palm Beach Lakes High School at Sheraton Hotel ballroom. Security guards found nail-studded bomb ready to be detonated in midst of five hundred students.
Result: Bomb destroyed and prom cancelled

Where: Port Huron, Michigan
When: May 18, 1999
Who: Jedaiah Zinzo, fourteen and Justin Schnepp, fourteen
What: Planned to outdo Columbine incident by raping girls and shooting up to 154 people on a targeted list. Plotted to force their principal at gunpoint to call an assembly, then massacre those at the gathering.

Result: Plan uncovered and students arrested. As of the publication of this book, the teens were ordered to stand trial on charges of conspiracy to commit murder.

Where: Minturn, Colorado
When: May 18, 1999
Who: Eighth-grade, fourteen-year-old female student
What: Told other students she planned to shoot up the school
Result: Student sent to psychiatric hospital

NOTES

CHAPTER 2

1. "Why the young kill," *Newsweek*, 3 May 1999, 35.
2. Ira J. Hadnot, "Violence begetting violence," *The Dallas Morning News*, 25 April 1999, 1J.

CHAPTER 3

1. "Games are no problem to this crowd," *USA Today*, 14 May 1999.
2. "Chemistry of a killer: Is it in the brain?" *USA Today*, 29 April 1999, 2A.
3. "Why the young kill," *Newsweek*, 3 May 1999, 34.
4. Ibid., 32.
5. Ibid., 33.
6. Pastor Dave Hart, Internet posting, 21 April 1999, http://tolos@cts.com.

CHAPTER 4

1. *American Family Association Journal*, June 1999, 7.
2. *The Black Flame*, Volume 6, Numbers 1 & 2, 5
3. *Rolling Stone*, 24 June 1999, 23.

4. Ibid., 77.

5. *AFA Journal,* June 1999, 24.

6. "Clinton calls for violence probe, riles Hollywood," *USA Today,* 2 June 1999, 1A.

7. *New York Times,* 26 May 1999, B9.

8. *USA Today,* 7 June 1999, 1D.

9. Ibid.

10. Ibid.

11. *USA Today,* 29 April 1999, 15A.

CHAPTER 5

1. Jack Thompson, "Bloodlust Video Games Put Kids in the Crosshairs," *The Denver Post,* 30 May 1999, 1G.

2. *USA Today,* 7 June 1999, 1D.

CHAPTER 6

1. *Time,* 31 May 1999, 38.

2. "Portrait of a deadly bond," *Time,* 10 May 1999, 26.

3. Associated Press, 27 May 1999.

4. *USA Today,* 28 May 1999, 8A.

5. "Escaping from the darkness," *Time,* 21 May 1999, 44.

6. "Portrait of a deadly bond," *Time,* 10 May 1999, 26.

CHAPTER 7

1. *USA Today,* 27 April 1998, 3A.

2. *People,* 3 November 1997, 118.

3. Associated Press, AOL, 5 June 1998

4. Ibid.

5. *USA Today,* 12 June 1998, 4A.

6. *USA Today*, 15 June 1998, 4A.
7. *The Denver Post* (Associated Press), 6 October 1998, 14A.
8. *The New York Times*, 3 December 1997, A14.
9. *USA Today*, 23 March 1999, 3A.
10. *The Indianapolis Star and The News*, 5 June 1999.
11. *Time*, 17 May 1999, 54.

CHAPTER 8
1. "Just a Routine School Shooting," *Time*, 31 May 1999, 34.
2. *New York Times*, 3 June 1998, A12.
3. "Life in the Womb: What the Fetus Knows," *Psychology Today*, September/October, 1998, 44–47, 76.
4. *New York Times*, 3 June 1998, A12.
5. *Time*, 13 April 1998, 61.
6. Ibid., 58.
7. *USA Today*, 12 April 1999, 15A.
8. "Gift of intuition can help teens save themselves," *USA Today*, 19 May 1999, 9D.
9. *People*, 3 November 1999, p. 121.
10. *Time*, 1 June 1998, 43.

CHAPTER 9
1. Don Tapscott, *Growing Up Digital: The Rise of the Net Generation* (New York: McGraw-Hill, 1998).
2. "Teens use technology their way," *The Washington Post*, 24 April 1999, A1.
3. "Depression recognized more often," *The Denver Post*, 27 April 1999, 6E.
4. *Time*, 31 May 1999, 47.

CHAPTER 10

   1. *The Denver Post*, 27 April 1999, 7B.

   2. *Tampa Tribune*, 25 May 1999, 5.

CHAPTER 11

   1. "It's a God thing," *Rocky Mountain News*, 4 July 1999, 40A–41A.

   2. Ibid.

   3. Message by Darrell Scott to Church on the Rock, 27 June 1999, transcript of tape.

   4. Ibid.

ABOUT THE AUTHOR

BOB LARSON, a popular author, lecturer, and commentator, is the host of a daily one-hour radio show, *TALK-BACK with Bob Larson,* that is heard in approximately one hundred cities in the United States and Canada. Bob's incisive commentaries on current events are enhanced by a format of live callers and interesting guests. Larson also hosts a weekly television show, *Bob Larson in Action,* that is telecast to more than five hundred stations.

Larson is the author of twenty-seven books, including three best-selling novels—*Dead Air, Abaddon,* and *The Senator's Agenda*—as well as *Larson's Book of Spiritual Warfare, Larson's Book of Cults, Satanism: The Seduction of America's Youth, Straight Answers to the New Age, In the Name of Satan,* and *UFOs and the Alien Agenda.*

Larson has lectured in more than eighty countries and has appeared on such television shows as *Oprah, Donahue, Montel, Sally Jesse, CNBC Talk-Live, Larry King Live,* and *Politically Incorrect.*

OTHER BOOKS BY BOB LARSON

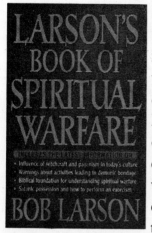

LARSON'S BOOK OF SPIRITUAL WARFARE

A comprehensive biblical guide into what actually motivates much of the deviant behavior behind today's headlines. This handbook discusses the occult and satanism in society, explains the scriptural basis for spiritual warfare, and gives information about demons and exorcism. Through reading this book, Christians will discover artillery they can use to effectively combat Satan's influence in today's culture.

0-7852-6985-1 • Trade Paperback • 504 pages

SATANISM: THE SEDUCTION OF AMERICAL'S YOUTH

Though many teenagers take Satan seriously, their parents often scoff at the idea of the devil. In *Satanism*, Bob Larson examines the pervasive influence of satanic activity on youth. More than just a simple overview of the dangers, this book provides practical ways to recognize and combat satanism.

0-8407-3034-9 • Trade Paperback • 224 pages

UFOs AND THE ALIEN AGENDA
Uncovering the Mystery Behind UFOs and the Paranormal

Many of today's top-grossing movies and top-rated TV shows are about extraterrestrials and the paranormal. Why is our culture so captivated by the possibility of life on other planets and alien life forms? In *UFOs and the Alien Agenda,* Bob Larson addresses such issues as: descriptions of close encounters with alien beings, the history of UFO sightings, the impact on Christians if life exists on other planets, how UFOs may fit into Satan's end-times deception, and what the Bible says about our culture's current quest to contact extraterrestrials. The alien "craze" is built on misinformation. *UFOs and the Alien Agenda* is the perfect place to start learning the truth about who is out there.

0-7852-7182-1 • Trade Paperback • 224 pages